YOUR PAST LIVES AND THE HEALING PROCESS

*A Psychiatrist Looks at
Reincarnation and Spiritual Healing*

by
Adrian Finkelstein, M.D.

50 Gates Publishing Company
Malibu, California
1996

"Something like this coming from a man of Dr. Finkelstein's reputation and training can help open minds. He should keep telling his stories."

— Bernie S. Siegel, M.D., Surgeon,
Founder and First President of The
American Holistic Medical Association,
Author of the bestseller: "Love,
Medicine and Miracles"

"Adrian Finkelstein writes from the heart. This book is a reflection of his deep caring for the emotional and spiritual healing of his patients."

— Bettye B. Binder, Teacher - Author,
President of The Association for Past-
Life Research & Therapies (APRT),
Riverside, California

"If the purpose of quality literature is to provoke ideas . . . and the goal is to be open to new paths for betterment and enlightenment then *Your Past Lives and the Healing Process* is a **milestone** work. I strongly recommend you read this integral work from a scientist, humanitarian and author of *A Psychiatrist's Search for GOD.*"

— Richard Fuller, Senior Editor,
Metaphysical Reviews,
Wyoming, Michigan

"In *Your Past Lives and the Healing Process*, Dr. Finkelstein shares with us his unique experiences with many amazing healing approaches and techniques. Therapists should thank Dr. Finkelstein for reminding us that a healer's heritage is as much Christ and Krishna as it is Freud and Jung, and therefore a healer's capacity to help is limited only by his spirit (which is limitless)."

— Krishan Bir, M.A., Ph.D.,
Former Chief Behavioral Therapist at
Montreal General Hospital, McGill
University, Montreal, Canada

"Dr. Adrian Finkelstein courageously has put forward his novel observations and experience of the world inside all of us. He has opened a whole new and unique psychiatric treatment technique."

— Said Rahban, M.D., F.A.C.P.,
Associate Clinical Professor,
Internal Medicine and Gastroenterology,
UCLA School of Medicine

YOUR PAST LIVES
AND THE
HEALING PROCESS

First printing January, 1985
Second printing, August, 1987
Second Edition, March, 1996

Manufactured in the United States of America by
50 Gates Publishing Company
P.O. Box 6090
Malibu, CA. 90264

ISBN 0-9647831-1-8

DEDICATION

To my family and to the world as a family.

ACKNOWLEDGEMENTS

I am deeply grateful to all the volunteers who participated in my research study, without whom this book would never have seen print. I am also indebted to those others who made this book possible, in particular, to Cliff Johnson, who undertook the lengthy and hard work of editing the manuscript and offered valuable recommendations. I am additionally thankful to Sheila Lodge, Carol Servi, and others who typed the manuscript and assisted me in my research. I certainly do not want to forget my good friends Dr. Arthur Altman and his wife, Susan, both of whom gave me constructive suggestions. Above all, final thanks go to my family who tolerated with love and understanding the hardship of my writing a book, especially my wife Parvaneh, my closest friend.

AUTIIOR'S NOTE

The following pages summarize the author's own research on reincarnation and spiritual healing and in no way does he undertake to represent any of the organizations or institutions he is affiliated with, nor is he endorsing any unrecognized treatment by the medical community in this country.

This book is not meant to offend, discredit, denigrate, or devaluate the medical profession, or other organizations or individuals, but rather to point to some insufficiently explored alternative or complimentary avenues in the philosophical approach to health, illness, and life in general.

CONTENTS

I. PAST LIVES

II. THE HEALING PROCESS

INTRODUCTION

Within the heart of every man and woman is the all-consuming desire for happiness. Without question it is this desire, elusive and indefinable as it is, which impels us to struggle against the limitations and imperfections of our lives. "I form light and create darkness, I make peace and create evil, I am G-d, I do all these things . . . Woe to the man who strives with his maker...." (Isaiah 45:7) Consciously or unconsciously, each of us is given free will and free choice, harkening to G-d's way to happiness, with His/Her promise of eternal peace and freedom. It seems to be G-d's intention in creating man and woman to give them the fundamental existential option of comparing. Only by comparing light with darkness or good with evil can one make this decision and thus exercise in this way one's freedom of choice.

We see the struggle for happiness occurring at three different levels. First, at the physical level. We yearn to be released from discomfort, hunger, the extremes of climate, and disease. We want a body free of pain. Second, we seek freedom from mental suffering—anguish, fear, boredom and, perhaps more today, the nervous anxiety that the complexities and accelerated pace of modern life have produced in us. We live in a largely discontented, stress-filled age. There is today a terrible lack of direction and faith. In spite of our material possessions, educational institutions and scientific advancements, we seem to have lost the radiance and gladness of life. Real joy has fled us because we have too often buried ourselves in senseless, vain activities that daily rob us of mental poise and therefore distract us from any serious internal searching. T.S. Eliot described it poignantly in these verses from *The Wasteland:*

"What shall I do now? What shall I do?"

"I shall rush out as I am, and walk the street With my hair down, so. What shall we do tomorrow? What shall we ever do."

The hot water at ten.
And if it rains, a closed car at four.
And we shall play a game of chess.
Pressing lidless eyes and waiting for a knock upon the
door.

The third level of our struggle, and by far the most significant—and subtle—is spiritual. Though not all of us may be consciously aware it, we seek ultimate freedom in G-d. With regard to this, we can make two preliminary statements: first, our spiritual nature is our *real* nature because it is the building material of our Soul, which is infinite and beyond change; second, this spirit is the source of all true and lasting happiness. It is this spiritual nature which makes us intuitively aware of the nature of true happiness, and, often unconsciously, is pressing us onward toward joy, bliss, and union with G-d.

If this desire for spiritual freedom is common to all of us, why then do not all of us actively seek union with G-d? Why do we continue to "play this empty play" with its endless rounds of false pleasures that we intuitively know can only, in the end, bring us pain?

It is because we have permitted ourselves to become deluded. Our delusion is a form of hypnotism, and the hypnotist is our own ego, which has convinced us that we require material success, recognition, and selfish enjoyments to be happy. These desires, prompted and sustained by the ego, have isolated us from G-D, the only source of true happiness. It is as simple as that—and as difficult.

Spinoza, in his essay, "On the Improvement of the Understanding," wrote of mankind's vain search for material and sensual happiness with telling insight:

> For the things which men, to judge by their actions, deem
> the highest good, are riches, fame, and sensual pleasure.
> Of these, the last is followed by satiety and repentance;
> the other two are never satiated. The more we have the
> more we want, while the love of fame compels us to order
> our lives by the opinions of others. But if a thing is not
> loved, no quarrels will arise concerning it, no sadness in
> short, no disturbances of the mind. All these spring from

the love of that which passes away; but the love of a thing
eternal and infinite fills the mind wholly with joy, and is
unmingled with sadness. Therefore, it is greatly to be
desired and to be sought with all our strength.[1]

A superficial reading of Spinoza might cause us to ask with
a shade of skepticism: "What is *really* wrong with desire? Must
I deny myself the good things of life in order to be spiritual?
What kind of G-d is it that apparently creates a world for our
enjoyment and then asks that we deny it?"

The answer lies in the kinds of desires that drive us. If they
are selfish—the type to which Spinoza obviously refers, those
that are driven by egotism—then we will ultimately suffer the
pain of dissatisfaction. To grow in spiritual happiness means
nothing less than the giving up of egotism or self-centeredness.

If we lack discrimination between what is pleasurable and
what is good or wise, it is extremely difficult to avoid some
kind of painful experience. Why? Because the mind that does
not discriminate is not able to recognize that everything to
which it is drawn contains a mixture of both pleasure and pain.
Over every office promotion hovers the threat of eventual
dismissal or demotion; every love affair, no matter how intense
in the beginning, may someday be tainted by jealousy or
boredom; and the inevitable hangover awaits the person who
drinks too much.

The secret is detachment. It is then we can truly enjoy this
bountiful world. Who enjoys a concert most—the orchestra or
the audience? The musicians are intent upon following the score
and the directions of the conductor. They are involved in the
"business" of playing. But members of the audience can sit
back and thoroughly enjoy the music, even though they might
know far less about it.

This universe is a mighty symphony which we can enjoy if
we learn to be good observers. Once we have learned to be the
director and not the directed in the various situations that life
presents to us, we will have taken the first and most important
step toward inner peace and harmony. And this also means
that our attitude toward religion must, in the case of most of
us, undergo a radical change. We must start to regard it as
something more than a social institution or as a subject fit only

for discussion or controversy. Religion must enter the very fabric of our lives, determine its ultimate values and shape the direction of our lives. However, as one of India's foremost philosopher, S. Radhakrishnan, writes:

> Humanism is the religion of the majority of the intellectuals of today. Most of whom profess to be religious by habit, sentiment or inertia. We accept our religion even as we do the Bank of England or the illusion of progress. We profess faith in G-d but are not inclined to act on it. We know the forms of thought but do not have the substance of conviction.[2]

Somehow this lack of conviction, this inertia, the terrible indifference we have developed toward religion must be changed. We can take our first step by recognizing that one of the primary problems of modern life is not disease or poverty, but spiritual ignorance. It is certainly true that religion will have no meaning for us if we suffer from the pangs of hunger or pain of an illness. But does this mean that these must be our *only* concerns? Will the cure of disease or hunger bring lasting happiness? Unfortunately, we will only hunger and become ill again. The real food for mankind is spiritual, and ultimately none of us will find true satisfaction with anything less.

I. PAST LIVES

CHAPTER ONE
Beginnings in the Search

About twenty-eight years ago I began experimenting with hypnosis. I was a medical student at the time and I was impressed by Dr. Dan Medina's hypnotic induction. Dr. Medina, a psychologist at Tel Hashomer Hospital in Tel Aviv, Israel, was involved in studies in the Memory Research Unit. He had been quite successful in hypnotically treating patients afflicted with bronchial asthma and other "psychosomatic" illnesses. Intrigued with hypnosis, I once asked Dr. Medina to hypnotize me so that I might experience it. This he did, and I felt a sort of magical, immensely enjoyable sensation descend upon me.

Shortly thereafter, I went back to the Department of Internal Medicine at the Hadassah Medical School in Jerusalem and continued the lengthy and strenuous task of observing my numerous patients. I felt they could benefit from hypnosis. At the time they were being treated by other therapeutic means — some without significant success; others ending in failure. My own subconscious programming in medical school had distracted me for a long time from that open-mindedness so I needed to probe the truth. I had learned a great many things from my patients, professors, textbooks, and laboratory tests, but little about holistic health. Only fragmentary bits of information had been given me, which only created bewilderment and uncertainty. Something was missing.

Eventually, I got my hands on *The Interpretation of Dreams* by Sigmund Freud. I read it and reread it avidly. It made me understand better the relationship between dreams and symptoms, whether they were emotional or physical. Dream symbolism fascinated me. I could see so convincingly, through Freud's interpretation of dreams, the interrelationship between mind and body.

Dr. I.I. Groen, the head of the Department of Medicine at the Hadassah Hospital in Jerusalem, had a profound influence on me. He was a wonderful teacher and physician who emphasized the psychosomatic approach to medicine. He believed in good "bed manners." I liked medicine, but I especially liked its psychosomatic aspects. The time came when I was torn between two choices in specialization: internal medicine or psychiatry. The latter prevailed. After graduating from Hadassah Medical School, I decided to train in psychiatry in the United States, where this specialty was more widely accepted than in Israel.

Though I was married, and with a child at the time, I embarked upon the path of hard training, finally graduating from the Menninger School of Psychiatry in Topeka, Kansas. This specialization in psychiatry gave me some psychoanalytic and research skills, and brought me closer to my conception of truth. I used dream analysis and hypnosis to establish the influence of mind over matter, and wrote articles on the subject. My studies were recognized by many of my colleagues, and this encouraged me to continue my research; but something was still missing.

Arriving in Chicago, I accepted the directorship of the Outpatient Psychiatric Department at the Mount Sinai Medical Center. I was soon to realize, however, that my training was insufficient to help a large number of my patients. What was really required, I thought, was an empathic, humanitarian approach, and I decided to go into private practice.

As I was still infatuated with psychoanalytic theory, I undertook personal analysis for about 700 hours with a training analyst at the Psychoanalytic Institute in Chicago. This training, perhaps more than any other, helped me become more sensitive to my patients' problems. It helped me to be more observant and tolerant, and certainly less critical of both my patients and medical students. That experience made me keenly aware of facts that are connected with the genetic explanation of psychological conflicts in this lifetime. It took years until I finally decided to acknowledge that even backed by such a powerful approach as psychoanalysis, I could not accomplish what I wanted - to really *help* people. It always seemed I would fall short of my expectations in assisting many of my patients, in spite of empathizing profoundly with them. Indeed, many times I didn't know what to do to help them in becoming self-sufficient and able to solve their own problems.

As the years went by, I continued to use hypnosis. At times I combined it with behavioral modification therapy as well as psychoanalytic psychotherapy. The pressure to conform to more accepted methods increased as most of my colleagues in psychiatry ended up using somatic approaches to treat psychiatric ailments. They were quick to explain to me that we live in a society that is becoming increasingly more accountable for the deeds of others; therefore, we, as physicians, must also become more accountable to the general public for the services we render. As a consequence, they said, psychiatry must be reoriented into the mainstream of medicine where more concrete methods of diagnosis and treatment are used. As a result, I began to invest more of my time and energy into studying more organic therapies. I began to treat more and more patients with medications, according to what I was taught.

Soon, however, I started seriously questioning what I had learned throughout those long years of study in medicine and psychiatry. I believed sincerely that psychoanalysis was a wonderful tool for many people, but it is a lengthy therapy involving great financial sacrifice, and there is the very great possibility that one may not find out all there is to know about oneself.

The time was soon to come when I realized that there was a great deal more to hypnosis than I had previously thought. Throughout my long experience with it, I discovered that certain habits such as smoking, nervous tics, lack of self confidence, minor "psychosomatic" ills, and the like, can be removed through hypnosis. This discovery came to me through many painful experiences; I began to feel that all the time, money and energy I had invested in other systems of treatment were in many cases futile or not very productive.

One day, while making notes on one of my dreams, I experienced a strange, almost eerie revelation. I felt as though I were in a state between sleep and waking, that I was a middle-aged woman doctor or healer, unmarried, quite ugly, but with a good heart. I "knew" that I liked to help my patients. My father was a carpenter. In this state I could see him most clearly, and after a while I even got the name of the country (Iran) and my name (Thelma Sangiavi). It was revealed to me that I had an impressive emotional experience at the time of my death (from a form of cancer). I could see a bright glowing light, and I sensed myself leaving my body. Then everything was gone. I opened my eyes and found it difficult to believe what I had experienced. Almost immediately it occurred to me that this must have been a past life, and I continued to search within myself as to whether or not I may have had other lives. Over a period of several months, I regressed myself through self-hypnosis into other lives in which I was both male and female. I began to trace a noticeable pattern throughout these so-called "past lives," a pattern that was remarkably similar to my behavior in this life. I was able to identify a total of eighteen past lives, eleven of them as male in different nonmedical or nonhealing occupations, and seven as a healer, or medical doctor. Two of these were as a female.

I also began a tentative quest into the subject of regression sometime prior to these experiences. I decided to read more in the literature of past-life regression and separate fact from fiction. In Raymond Moody's book *Life After Life*, I found an impressive gathering of over one hundred reports of near-death experiences, reported by patients he interviewed. But I felt the evidence was still insufficient to answer the question of whether another life does exist, or whether he only presents a glimpse into a possible existence hereafter. Dr. Elizabeth Kubler-Ross's work, *On Death and Dying*, was also instrumental in my further pursuit of this line of investigation.

Some time prior to my digging into past lives, I became interested in the phenomenon of ESP. I began to analyze my dreams to determine my own degree of extrasensory perception. Often I could identify in them the precognition of certain events. My experience with precognition started early in life, when I was about two years old in Bucharest, Romania. During one night I cried a great deal and made such a fuss about sleeping in my own bed that my parents took me into theirs. That night Romania experienced a catastrophic earthquake. Stones and bricks filled my empty bed. Precognition had saved my life.

During the second World War, when I was six years of age, I went with my parents to the air raid shelter during bombing raids. I could hear the bombs falling. I remember how tense my body was in fright on hearing the shrill sound of a falling bomb. Between the wooden studs of the shelter, I could clearly see the fire of the explosions. To the amazement of all, the bombs would stop falling when I would count to three. Quite often, people in the shelter would ask me to begin counting, and "magically," most of the time, the bombs would stop. Occasionally, I would tell them to wait for a while; afterwards, I would count successfully.

One day, when I was nine, I was with my mother at my school for the final examination at the end of third grade. My mother waited across the street in a public park. I left her to go over to the school to discover when the examination was to begin. As I ran back to tell my mother the news, a truck, driving on the wrong side of the street, struck me. At the last moment I remember seeing the grill on the front of the engine. Then, it seems, I found myself up in the air, several yards in front of the vehicle, watching myself from the back as I was hanging on the grill. The next thing I recall was being carried in my teacher's arms. It was Professor Almoslino, the art teacher, and he took me to the nearest hospital. I was told that I had some cracked ribs. Afterwards, my parents told me I passed out as I fell between the wheels of the truck, which miraculously passed over me without touching my body. I attribute this to my subconscious intuition, which perceived myself hanging by my hands in the middle of the engine's grill of that truck. My amazing out-of-body experience made sense to me after reading Dr. Moody's book about near-death experiences.

When I was about ten or eleven, I told my parents that the dog belonging to Aunt Fanny gave birth to eight puppies. That same day my parents asked my aunt if it were true. She denied it. As a result, my parents scolded me for telling a lie. Then I told them I meant that the dog will give birth to eight puppies. On the following day it did, indeed, give birth to eight puppies.

Many years later I provided myself with another example of a parapsychological experience - astral travel. I put myself into a state of hypnosis and decided to travel from Chicago to Israel, to my parents-in-law, and see what they were doing. It was about 4:00 p.m. Chicago time, which meant midnight in Israel. I found my mother-in-law in her kitchen, bent over the sink, washing dishes, and my father-in-law in a room adjacent to the kitchen. I came out of my state of trance and told my wife what I had experienced. Naturally, she was skeptical and proposed that we immediately call them and find out if what I had seen was true. The call confirmed everything I had witnessed.

11

I have been made aware that in my practice whenever I operate intuitively, using more my "feel" for the patient's problem rather than my scientific approach, I get much better results. I can then see how a patient improves under my very eyes and remains well thereafter. After 28 years of working with hypnosis, I decided there were two important factors which determine the difference between failure and success: self-help and a positive mental attitude. I made the point of carefully explaining to each of my patients what I meant by self-help. I would sometimes cite the Scandinavian proverb, "If I give you a fish today, you will not be hungry today - but what about tomorrow? It is better I show you how to fish." I taught people self-hypnosis, a concentrated form of self-help, by which they could better tune themselves into their subconscious. The primary, purpose is to "favorably" reprogram the subconscious and thereby alter its influence on the conscious mind. Though the self-hypnosis exercise lasts only one minute, it must be repeated ten to twenty times each day. Intuitively, I felt through my clinical practice that this was the correct number, as there are correct doses of medication. The results have been immensely encouraging.

We are bombarded throughout our everyday life by a great number of negatives. It is no wonder the subconscious will sooner or later feed back negative information to us. By, the same token, repeatedly bombarding the subconscious with positives through self-hypnosis, we can create positive reactions from the subconscious.

It is a well-known psychological fact that learning takes place best when it is repeated often and for brief periods of time. But learning does not simply mean feeding material or information to the subconscious; it also implies the manner in which the subconscious is fed, the motivation and energy that are invested in the process. I explain all this to my patients, and whenever they take advantage of this information they improve amazingly.

The other important factor is a positive mental attitude. Through experience I discovered that thoughts are extremely powerful. But a thought, like a fine motor car, cannot run without gas — or energy. Thought has a body: it is like a mold. It depends on whether or not this mold is filled with energy in the form of emotion, motivation, or will power for it to become action. Negative thoughts made up of emotions such as fear, worry, depression, and the like, will sooner or later translate into negative action. Again, it is not enough to simply construct a thought. The energy put into that thought, into that suggestion or affirmation, makes all the difference between success and failure. In addition, visualization of the outcome is essential, as the subconscious, like a young child, understands pictures better than words. What one thinks, one creates. What one feels, one attracts. What one imagines, one becomes!

The very essence of self-help and positive mental attitude simply means to take full responsibility for oneself and have full faith in G-d or the higher power working through oneself. I often point out to my patients the importance of taking full responsibility for whatever happens to them, and not to blame it on the other guy. Unfortunately, we live in a society that is often in a state of turmoil and confusion, and it is far easier to blame the other person than assume full responsibility for one's own deeds. There is a wise saying: "When you point a finger at someone, three fingers point back at you". Peace, prosperity, and happiness come from within the individual. It is a fallacy to maintain that it should come from outer conditions. War invites war; peace and love invite peace and love.

With this interest in hypnosis as a background, I began to develop an interest in psychic healing. I sought to discover objectively whether such healings were true or false. I was initially intrigued with the accounts of healings performed by Tony Agpaoa, a Filipino psychic surgeon, who literally penetrated into the human body with his bare hands. He would remove a tumor or portion of the sick tissue within seconds or minutes, healing an individual who could often not be helped by conventional methods.

At first I looked upon such "surgery" with great suspicion. My own scientific attitude, which was formed in my subconscious, particularly during my academic training, prevented me from making much sense of such healing. Also, several published reports on psychic surgery were quite negative; but my intuition kept telling me that in spite of such reports, it was true. Because my intuition had served me well before, particularly when combined with my reason, I decided to personally investigate the matter. I wrote a letter to Rosita Rodriguez, the closest collaborator of Tony Agpaoa. She lived not far from me in Oak Park, Illinois, and I thought if she would accept an interview, I would have a golden opportunity to discuss some of these methods and thereby satisfy my curiosity.

As she was abroad in the Philippines, it took some time until I could meet her. While waiting for an answer, I continued my research into past lives, which I had been quietly conducting for about two or three years.

After several hundred regressions, I finally understood that to scientifically prove the validity of any other life besides the present one, I had to spend a number of hours with each subject. Personal data had to be carefully examined for future verification. Therefore, the final one hundred cases of past-life regression under hypnosis or through guided imagery, I performed with an emphasis on facts that could stand the test of genealogical research.

CHAPTER TWO:
Reincarnation: A History and Profile

For thousands of years, the Phoenix bird has been a symbol for rebirth. According to legend, the phoenix lived for five or six hundred years in the Arabian wilderness, after which it would burn itself on a funeral pyre, then rise from the ashes, fresh and youthful, and live through another cycle of years. A glowing spark, signifying immortality, would always remain, and from it a new life was initiated.

During the Middle Ages, a legend circulated in a collection of Christian stories called *Physiologus*, relating to the animal kingdom. People read them with enormous interest, in spite of their being banned by the Church. In the *Physiologus*, the Phoenix is envisioned as an Indian bird that subsists on air for five hundred years, then flies to Egypt, where it appears in the temple at Heliopolis, and is burned to ashes on the altar. The following day a young, feathered Phoenix is already developing, and on the third day is fully grown. After saluting the priest, it flies away.

The ancient Irish thought their own Phoenix had a longevity of six hundred years. The Turks called theirs *kerkes*, and the Japanese, *kirin*. According to the Turks, kerkes lives a thousand years. Herodotus, the famous historian, observed that the Phoenix was one of the sacred birds or hieroglyphics of the Egyptians. It can often be found in *The Book of the Dead*, where it is called the *benu* bird.

It is interesting to note in this context that Hegel, the nineteenth-century German philosopher, believed that reincarnation was the highest metaphysical idea in the Oriental tradition, and one that emphasized growth and purification through the consecutive cycles of life.

Because of its periodic renewal, the snake has become another symbol of renewal. The emblem of the medical profession came from the mythological symbolism found in Caduceus, the serpent of Hermes and Mercury. There is a famous 700-foot serpent mound in Ohio, in which the snake bears an egg in its mouth. In other positions the serpent is shown swallowing its tail, signifying the eternity circle of life without beginning or end. The wisdom of the serpent resides in his knowledge of both life and death.

According to the Hindu belief, *Manvatara* is that period of evolution stretching from the beginning of time to its end, and consists of a journey, not only from birth to death, but throughout millions of years. Since the Hindus consider man to be a spiritual being, the continuity of his existence is uninterrupted. Experience through the ladder of reincarnation extends from the very bottom to the top. In one life a man may be wealthy and powerful, but in another, a slave or a pauper.

Life after death is universally accepted in the Orient; philosophers and religious teachers seldom felt the need to prove this belief. Hindu and Buddhist writings are never quite the same, but their mutual agreement on rebirth clearly communicates a central theme of eternal growth. In a boundless universe, they aver, there should be innumerable possibilities for growth, wisdom, selfrealization, and attainment of higher levels of consciousness. Buddha believed in divine but wholly practical wisdom. He said, "Bear always in mind what it is that I have not elucidated and what it is that I have elucidated - I have not elucidated that the world is eternal, I have not elucidated that the world is not eternal, I have not elucidated that the saint exists after death, I have not elucidated that the saint both exists and does not exist after death. And what have I elucidated? Misery - the origin of misery -the cessation of misery - the path leading to the cessation of misery."[3]

In the Judeo-Christian belief there are also references to reincarnation. A biblical reference that may imply reincarnation is found in *Psalms* 90:3-6, which emphasizes a thousand-year cycle between incarnations. The Jews expected the return of their great prophet, and according to scholar Rabbi Moses Gaster, the belief is that Adam returned as Seth, then as Noah, Abraham, and Moses. There is also one claim that Adam was reincarnated as David and will still come back as the Messiah. In the New Testament there is strong evidence of an expectation among the people that the prophets would return.

Isaac Myer's noted work on the *Kabala* provides a long list of Europeans who believed to some degree in reincarnation. This included Jacob Boehme, Ficino Pico, Pope Sixtus, Raymond

Lully, Cornelius Agrippa, John Raechlin, Spinoza, Leibniz, Ralph Cudworth, Henry More, Francis Bacon, Isaac Newton, as well as the philosophers Schopenhauer, Hegel, and Schelling. In attempting to answer the intriguing question as to where the ancient Jews originally obtained these teachings, Myer writes, "The Quabbalah most likely originally came from the Aryan sources through Central Asia, Persia, India, and Mesopotamia, or from Urharhan, came Abraham and many others into Palestine."[4] We know that the Hebrew Genesis and many parts of the old Testament are tinged with the Aryan, Akkadian, Chaldean, and Babylonian cultures. And there is evidence that Isaiah, Daniel, Ezra, Jeremiah, Ezekiel, and other Israelites were under the influence of Persian and Chaldean learning. There are several references to the wisdom of sages of the East in the Hebrew Sacred Writings, for communication between the ancient nations of Asia was much more general than has been usually thought.

In one of the most controversial passages in the Bible, Christ offers a strong indication of having lived before: "Who do men say I the son of man am?" he asked his disciples.

"And they said, some say that you are John the Baptist, some Elijah, and others Jeremiah, or one of the prophets." (Matthew 16:13-14)

Another striking instance of a Biblical reference to reincarnation again occurs in the Book of Matthew when Jesus is transfigured before Peter, James and John. "As they came down from the mountain, Jesus charged them, saying, "Tell the vision to no man until the Son of man be risen again from the dead.

"And his disciples asked him, saying, Why then say the scribes that Elias must first come?

"And Jesus answered and said unto them, Elias truly shall come first, and restore all things.

"But I say unto you that Elias is come already, and they knew him not, but have done unto him whatsoever they listed. Likewise shall also the Son of man suffer of them.

"Then the disciples understood that he spake unto them of John the Baptist." (Matthew 17:9-13)

Jesus was once questioned concerning a man who had been born blind. "Who did sin, this man or his parents?" his disciples

17

asked him. Jesus replied that the man was afflicted because he was destined by Christ to have his sight restored so that "the works of G-d should be made manifest in him." (John 9:2,3) He leaves us with reincarnation as the only option to explain the cause of blindness at birth.

In still another instance that indicates the operation of the law of *karma,* or cause and effect, Christ warned that "they who take the sword shall perish with the sword." (Matthew 26:52) Again, such an admonition is strongly suggestive of acceptance by Jesus of a philosophy of rebirth.

Reincarnation appears in the Islamic tradition as well. Basically, the position adopted by the successors of Mohammed was to affirm the belief in reincarnation, but not to propagate it as a teaching for the masses. Acceptance of such a doctrine requires a subtle understanding of the higher plan of creation, which appears to have been either beyond the capacity of or of no interest to the early Islamic monarchs. As a result, the study of reincarnation was largely left to the students of Sufism, the mystical sect of Islam. It is interesting to note, however, that a Muslim is in no danger of being accused of heresy if he accepts reincarnation.

According to some authorities, a number of esoteric schools of Islam accept three types of rebirth: *Hulul,* the periodic incarnation of a Perfect Being or Deity; *Rij'at,* the return of the Imam or spiritual leader after death; and *Tansukh,* which refers to the rebirth of the souls of ordinary men.[5]

The Ismailis, or Shiah sect, have gone as far as to announce that the Hindu deity Krishna progressively reincarnated as Buddha and then Mohammed. And one of the Rafziah sects affirms that "at no time is the world left without a Teacher as a guide, that is, some person or other ... His great soul is manifesting all the time."[6]

In the Koran we find several references to reincarnation. These two are representative: "As the rains turn the dry earth into green, thereby yielding fruits, similarly G-d brings the dead into life so that thou mayest learn." (*Sura Iraf-Meccan,* 8:6-6-13) "(Those who doubt immortality) are dead and they do not know when they will be born again. Your G-d is peerless, and those who have no faith in the ultimate have perverse hearts and they want to pose as great men." (*Sura Nahel,* 14:2-12-8)

Primitive man, as well, found that reincarnation provided him with an acceptable and rational answer to many of the mysteries of life. Most Africans, for example, view reincarnation as something basically "good," for it means a return to a better, more vigorous life. They appear to have no conception of an end to the number of births, and consider it unfortunate not to be reborn. Hence, childlessness is a great curse, for it interrupts the cycle of rebirth. Africans pay great heed to fertility, and generally practice polygamy, for the belief is that an ancestor is only reincarnated in his own family. The most popular mystery for them to solve is the identity of the ancestor incarnated in a newborn infant.

Natives of the Pacific Islands have also maintained a strong historic belief in reincarnation. Typical is that held by the Okinawans, who accept the human being as possessing a spirit which leaves the body at death and later returns to earth as a newborn infant. The belief is that the spirit remains in its "home" — the deceased body — for forty-nine days, at which time it enters a *Gusho* or place beyond the material world.

The period between lives varies, but Okinawans believe that the spirit will return within seven generations to an individual who strongly resembles his former embodiment. Not all beings reincarnate. Some remain in Gusho and greet new arrivals to that state. It should be borne in mind that the Okinawan view of Gusho is that of a spiritual realm or state where only the spirit of man exists. It is the spirit that reincarnates, not the mind. Mind is received by the individual through ancestral descent.[7]

The Okinawan belief system appears to have produced some positive benefits in terms of mental health. A study of some 500 Okinawans following World War II revealed that only one of them became mentally unstable as a result of sustained heavy bombardment during the war, a terrible ordeal that drove numerous Japanese to suicide and many American soldiers into mental wards. The reason for such stability appears to lie with the rearing of Okinawan children, who have a well-developed sense of security by the time they are five. Thus, they have a mental foundation strong enough to survive upheavals. And since the child is less programmed by false beliefs, it has, in a sense, developed a wisdom far beyond his years. Thus, it would appear that a belief in reincarnation contributes to mental stability.[8]

In her investigations of the Eskimos and Balinese, anthropologist Margaret Mead discovered that both cultures accepted reincarnation, which apparently led them to attribute prophetic powers to infants, who are taught complex skills quite early in life.

Similar concepts of reincarnation exist among several tribes of the American Indians or Native Americans as well, especially among the tribes of the Eastern United States. The Lenape tribe of Delaware and New Jersey claim that several members of their tribe— the "pure in heart" — have the ability to recall former lives.[9]

A number of other tribes, notably the Pueblos, seem to have little or no regard for the body after death, believing as they do that the soul will go to a next life and build for itself a new and better body.

While digging near Otowl, New Mexico, archeologist Weshe Bradford found a jar beneath an ancient house containing the skeleton of an infant. An Indian woman from a neighboring tribe told him that from ancient times her people believed that a baby taken by death would return to the same family if the body were buried beneath the ancestral home, enabling the soul to more easily find it.[10]

The ancient Greeks found sympathy with many of these ideas. They believed the soul to be divine and immortal, ever struggling to attain freedom from the body, which holds it prisoner. Death dissolves the physical body, but the soul is again captured in another body as the wheel of rebirth moves on. This Orphic belief appears to have been widely disseminated among the Greek colonies of South Italy and Sicily.

It is interesting to note that one of history's most famous Greeks, Aristotle, accepted the doctrine of rebirth as a young man, but in later years rejected such a concept because he considered the soul to have no capacity to recollect previous lives.[11]

The Romans, as well, expressed similar arguments in favor of karma and rebirth through the mouth of the famous orator, Cicero: "The ancients, whether they were seers, or interpreters of the divine mind in the tradition of the sacred initiations, seem to have known the truth, when they affirmed that we were born into the body to pay the penalty for sins committed in a former life." And in his dialogue, "On Old Age," he states:

> The soul is of heavenly origin, forced down from its home in the highest, and, so to speak, buried in earth, a place quite opposed to its divine nature and its immortality . . . Nor is it only reason and argument that have brought me to this belief, but the great fame and authority of the most distinguished philosophers. I used to be told that Pythagoras and the Pythagoreans - almost natives of our country, who in old times had been called the Italian School of Philosophers - never doubted that we had souls drafted from the universal Divine Intelligence.
>
> I used besides to have pointed out to me the discourse delivered by Socrates on the last day of his life upon the immortality of his soul - Socrates . . . the wisest of men, I need say no more. I have convinced myself, and I hold in view of the rapid movement of the soul, its vivid memory of the past and its prophetic knowledge of the future, its many accomplishments, its vast range of knowledge, its numerous discoveries - that a nature embracing such varied gifts cannot itself be mortal. Since the soul is always in motion and yet has no external source of motion, for it is self-moved. I conclude that it will also have no end to its motion, because it is not likely ever to abandon itself . . .
>
> It is again a strong proof of men knowing most things before birth, that when mere children they grasp innumerable facts with such speed as to show that they are not then taking them in for the first time, but remembering and recalling them.[12]

Julius Caesar found the Celts to be remarkably fearless in battle. Apparently investigating the reasons for this, he wrote: "They wish to inculcate this as one of their leading tenets, that souls do not become extinct, but pass after death from one body to another, and they think that men by this tenet are in a great degree excited to valor, the fear of death being disregarded."[13]

21

Dante's Divine Comedy, presents a vivid description of purification, purgatory and sublimation in heaven that offers a clue to reason for the soul's return to Earth. In Canto XX of *Paradiso*, Dante writes of meeting a Roman emperor in the Heaven of Jupiter, and being told "He from Hell came back into his bones, and this was the reward of living hope — the living hope which put power into the prayers made to G-d to raise him up, that his will might be moved. The glorious soul returning to flesh where it abode awhile, believed in Him who had power to help, the believing, kindled into such a flame of Love, that at the second death it was worthy to come into this joy."

We know that other distinguished men of that era, such as Leonardo da Vinci, Paracelsus, and Jordano Bruno, believed in reincarnation. In Sonnet 59, Shakespeare ponders it:

If there be nothing new, but that which is
Hath been before, how are our brains beguil'd,
Which labouring for invention, bear amiss
The second burthen of a former child!

Among the doctors of the mind, American psychologist and philosopher William James was one of the most significant to share an interest in reincarnation. At Harvard, in 1893, he delivered his famous Ingersoll lecture, "Human Immortality," in which he affirmed that physiological psychology did indeed accept a scientific basis for immortality. These findings, he said, rested on the reductionist view that the brain functions only in a protective thinking capacity. But he stressed that the brain can just as easily transmit ideas that have an origin elsewhere. He argued that when the brain finally ceases to function, it will vanish from the observable world; but the sphere of being that *supplies* consciousness will still exist. Consciousness might, in ways unknown to us, still continue, he said. In the preface to his second edition, James expanded on these concepts and spoke of reincarnation.

Many critics have made one and the same objections to the doorway of immortality which his lecture claims to be left open by his "transmission theory" of cerebral action. James believes in an infinite mundane consciousness in which the brain is seen as a transmissive organ.

> If our finite personality here below, the objectors say,
> be due to the transmission through the brain of portions
> of a pre-existing larger consciousness, all that can remain
> after the brain expires is the larger consciousness itself
> as such. But this, the critics continue, is the pantheistic
> idea of immortality, survival, namely, in the soul of the
> world, not the Christian idea on immortality, which
> means survival in strictly personal form
> The plain truth is that one may conceive the mental
> world behind the veil in as individualistic a form as one
> pleases, without any detriment to the general scheme by
> which the brain is represented as a transmissive organ.
> If the extreme individualistic view were taken, one's finite
> mundane consciousness would be an extract from one's
> larger, truer personality, the latter having even now some
> sort of reality behind the scenes...
> It is true that all this would seem to leave affinities with
> pre-existence and with possible reincarnation than with
> the Christian notion of immortality. But my concern in
> the lecture was not to discuss immortality in general with
> the brain-function theory of our present mundane
> consciousness. I hold that it is compatible, and
> compatible moreover in fully individualized form. The
> reader would be in accord with everything that the text
> of my lecture intended to say, were he to assert that every
> memory and affection of his present life is to be preserved,
> and that he shall never in *saecula, saeculorum* cease to be
> able to say to himself: "I am the same personal being who
> in old times upon the earth had those experiences."[14]

Sigmund Freud, as well, spoke extensively of immortality
in his article, "Thoughts for the Times on War and Death,"
written during World War I. He wrote:

> To anyone who listened to us (in the West), we were
> prepared to maintain that death was the necessary
> outcome of life . . . In reality, however, we showed an
> unmistakable tendency to put death on one side, to
> eliminate it from life . . . The complement to this cultural

and conventional attitude towards death is provided by our complete collapse when death has struck down someone whom we love . . . But this attitude . . . towards death has a powerful effect on our lives. Life is impoverished . . . when the highest stake in the game of living, life itself, may not be risked . . . We dare not contemplate a great many undertakings which are dangerous . . .

It is an inevitable result of all this that we should seek in the world of literature and in the theatre, compensation for what has been lost in life . . . In the realm of fiction we find the plurality of lives which we need. We die with the hero . . . yet we survive him and are ready to die again just as safely with another hero . . .

When primeval man saw someone who belonged to him die . . . then in his pain, he was forced to learn that one can die, too, and his whole being revolted against the admission . . . So he devised a compromise; he considered the fact of his own death . . . but denied the significance of annihilation . . . His persisting memory of the dead became the basis for assuming other forms of existence and gave him the conception of a life continuing after apparent death.

These subsequent existences were at first no more than appendages to the existence which death had brought to a close — shadowy, empty of content, and valued at little . . . After this it was no more than consistent to extend life backwards into the past, to form a notion of earlier existences, of the transmigration of souls and of reincarnation, all with the purpose of depriving death of its meaning as the termination of life . . . It was only later that religions succeeded in representing (the) after-life as the more desirable, the truly valid one . . . at bottom no one believes his own death, which amounts to saying: "In the unconscious every one of us is convinced of his own immortality." [15]

While Freud seems to speak with great assurance as to how primeval man thought, he had little scientific evidence to support his conjectures, considering that anthropologists now find man to be more than three-and-a-half million years old. Any personal speculations on this subject cannot help but expose the investigator's views as to the nature of man and his destiny.

It seems evident that the only possible clues to the way primitive man thought about immortality are to be found in his myth-symbols, whose tradition dates from a remote past. Freud seemingly tried to quiet modern man's fears of dying. But from where does such fear come? Apparently it was not known to the early races, for many of them such as the American Indian and the Eskimo, showed complete calm in the fact of death — at least until their cultures were interfered with by the white man!

In a conversation with Ludwig Binswanger, Freud surprised his friend and colleague by admitting that "mankind has always known that it possesses spirit: I had to show it that there are also instincts." Years later, when Binswanger delivered an address at Freud's eightieth birthday, the latter wrote him: "I've always lived only in the *parterre* (pit) and the basement of the building. You claim that with a change of viewpoint one is able to see an upper story which houses such distinguished guests as religion, art, etc. . . . If I had another lifetime of work before me, I have no doubt that I could find room for these noble guests in my little subterranean house."[16]

Another modern voice to join the controversy over immortality and rebirth was that of C. G. Jung. In *Memories, Dreams, and Reflections,* Jung wrote he had "never written expressly about a life after death," but said finally, he liked to state his ideas. "Perhaps one has to be close to death to acquire the necessary freedom to talk about it." He revealed that almost all his life he had pondered this problem and that all his works "are fundamentally nothing but attempts, ever renewed, to give an answer to the question of the interplay between the 'here' and the `hereafter.'"[17]

Many years earlier he had a commentary on an old Chinese book: "Death is psychologically just as important as birth, and . . . an integral part of life. It is not the psychologist who must be questioned as to what happens finally to the detached consciousness. Whatever theoretical position he assumed, he would hopelessly overstep the boundaries of his scientific

25

competence. He can only point out that the views of our text with respect to the timelessness of the detached consciousness, are in harmony with the religious thought of all times and with that of the overwhelming majority of mankind. He can say, further, that anyone who does not think this way would stand outside the human order, and would, therefore, be suffering from a disturbance in his psychic equilibrium. As a physician then, I make the greatest effort to fortify, so far as I have the power, a belief in immortality, especially in my older patients to whom such questions come menacingly near."[18]

The first revelation of Jung's interest in reincarnation comes from a lecture entitled "Concerning Rebirth," that he gave in 1939, and which he later revised in 1950. He began with an introduction to metempsychosis and reincarnation, and defined reincarnation in these words: "This concept of rebirth necessarily implies the continuity of personality. Here the human personality is regarded as continuous and accessible to memory, so that, when one is incarnated or born, one is able, at least potentially, to remember that one has lived through previous existences, and that these existences were one's own, i.e., that they had the same ego-form as the present life. As a rule, reincarnation means rebirth in a human body."

Jung continues, "Rebirth is the affirmation that must be counted among the primordial affirmations of mankind. These primordial affirmations are based on what I call archetypes . . ."[19]

During the latter part of the nineteenth century we find emerging in the West a new religious philosophy with mystical concerns that can be traced to the ancient world and which were to have a catalytic effect upon the decades to follow. The movement known as Theosophy was to be a pioneering agency in the promotion of greater Western acquaintance with Hindu and Buddhist thought. In the United States, alone, it has influenced a whole series of religious movements. It is the estimate of some scholars that no other single organization has done more to popularize the Asian religions and philosophical ideas in the West than Theosophy.

Reviewing Western thought prior to the 1870's, it becomes evident that many leading minds in the world of religion, science, philosophy, art, and literature, had almost, without exception, something stimulating to say on the subject of reincarnation. As to the masses, the teaching was nearly unknown from the time of the crusade against the widespread Christian Gnostic Cathari movement of the Middle Ages to perhaps the 1880's. Immediately prior to the Theosophical movement, Edward Tylor, the father of anthropology, could write in his renowned work, *Religion in Primitive Culture*, "We have traced the theory of metempsychosis in stage after stage of the world's civilization, scattered among the native races of America and Africa, established in the Asiatic nations ... rising and falling in classic and medieval Europe, and lingering at last in the modern world as an intellectual crotchet, of little account but to the ethnographer who notes it down, as an item of evidence for his continuity of culture."

What also appears in the religious renewal of the nineteenth century, he claims, is faith in an everlasting heaven, which provides "an answer to the perplexed problem of the allotment of happiness and misery in the present world, by the expectation of another world to set this right."[20]

What are modern Western beliefs regarding reincarnation? Although statistical information is relatively scarce, a 1969 Gallup Poll assessing the beliefs of twelve nations revealed the following percentage of persons who accepted a doctrine of reincarnation in these Western countries: Austria, 20%; Canada, 26%; France, 23%; Great Britain, 18%; Greece, 22%; the Netherlands, 25%. These figures are particularly interesting since neither Protestantism nor Catholicism teach acceptance of rebirth.

What is truly astonishing is that nearly twice the number of Americans who accepted reincarnation ten years ago believe in it today! A recent project by the Center of Para-analytical Studies in San Diego, California polled ten thousand Americans at random and discovered that 41 % of those questioned believed in reincarnation, 20 % expressed no belief in it, and 39 % were undecided.

My own clinical poll for three years, from 1990 to 1993, on over 400 patients revealed that over 70 % of them believe in reincarnation or are open to this idea, though they came to me usually due to anxiety or depression and were not aware of my work with reincarnation. It is interesting to note that in a survey published in the *Psychiatric Times* a few years ago, it was found that 60 % of women and 52 % of men suffer from intermediate and high anxiety, while 41 % of women and 34 % of men suffer from intermediate to deep depression representing most of the patient population in my own clinical poll.

CHAPTER THREE
Research into the Past

Dr. Ian Stevenson, a leading scientific investigator in the field of reincarnation, first became publicly known in 1960, when his "Evidences of Survival from Claimed Memories of Former Incarnations" received the winning prize in the contest of the American Society for Psychical Research. Prior to writing the essay, Stevenson had studied hundreds of cases in which children and adults appeared to remember their past lives. With only one exception, the claimed memories on which Dr. Stevenson bases his conclusions happened spontaneously in normal stages of consciousness. He states that the writer had the privilege of announcing his own personal interpretation of the data. He claims that reincarnation is the most plausible hypothesis for explaining the cases of this series. He does not conclude that they prove reincarnation either singularly or together; indeed, he is quite sure they do not.

In 1966, Stevenson published *Twenty Cases Suggestive of Reincarnation,* which is now considered a small classic in the field of reincarnation." Stevenson traveled to South America, Alaska, Europe, the Near East, Asia, and many parts of the United States to conduct an on-the-spot research into reported cases. His book is considered by most to be thoroughly scientific. Dr. Albert Stunkard, chairman of the department of psychiatry at the University of Pennsylvania, said: "Stevenson's present work . . . seems queer to many conventional scientists. It is certainly controversial. But he is the most critical man I know of working in that sphere, and perhaps the most thoughtful, with a knack for building into his research appropriate investigative controls." The article reports that Stevenson became interested in reincarnation because of a "growing feeling of dissatisfaction that available knowledge of heredity and environmental influences, considered either alone or together, often didn't account for personality as we see it."

In an interview *(National Enquirer,* December 17, 1967), Stevenson explained that in studying cases of reincarnation he employed the combined methods of a historian, lawyer, and psychiatrist. He gathered testimony from as many witnesses as he could; it was commonplace for him to interview twenty-five people with regard to a single case of reincarnation, and he has frequently returned to interview the same people several years later. According to Stevenson, he had to first eliminate the possibility of fraud, then to rule out any suggestion that the subject might have obtained, through word of mouth, a newspaper account or other source, details of the stranger he now claimed to have been in a previous life.

Finally, Stevenson had to eliminate the possibility that the subject may have obtained information by extrasensory means; telepathy, for instance. He remarked, however, that ESP cannot account for a subject having skills and talents not learned in this lifetime — such as the ability to speak a foreign language. Nor can it account for bizarre birthmarks that seem to relate to the prior life. Many of the cases involved individuals who recalled over twenty-five items from their past lives. These were later verified. Almost all of Stevenson's reports concern persons who in their former life died at an early age and reincarnated within a few years, enabling previous relatives still alive to confirm claimed recollections. All in all, Stevenson and his colleagues investigated about two hundred cases.

It is interesting to note that of the 1,339 reincarnation cases reported on file throughout the world as of July 1974, the United States possesses the majority - 324. Other countries are: Burma (139), India (135), Turkey (114), and Great Britain (111).

In the West, where reincarnation is not generally accepted, there is an unfortunate tendency to ignore, suppress, or ridicule revelations of children who seem compelled to talk about a time prior to their birth. Their statements are generally not taken seriously. The interpretation of such cases as examples of ESP does not seem adequate, since most of the subjects show no signs of being unusually gifted with this ability. If their past life memories are really only disguised extrasensory perceptions, why should this ability be displayed in such a specialized, narrow way? These children would in any event have to be credited with extraordinary abilities, indeed, to receive such a large number of correct details about the pertinent circumstances of a particular deceased person."[21]

In 1974, the University Press of Virginia published another Stevenson volume, *Xenoglossy*, which received considerable attention in the press. Xenoglossy is a word coined by an early parapsychologist referring to the ability to speak a language not learned in any normal way. Stevenson presents the case of Lydia Johnson (a pseudonym) who had consented to help her physician husband with experiments in hypnotism. She proved an excellent subject, capable of slipping easily into a deep trance. Her husband had learned hypnotism as an adjunct to his practice, thinking it might help in the treatment of some of his patients.

As the experiments with his wife progressed, Dr. Johnson decided to take his wife back into an earlier time through hypnotic regression. Suddenly Lydia flinched as if struck. She screamed, grabbed her head, and her husband quickly ended the session. But his wife was left with a headache that could not be understood. Twice Johnson repeated the session with similar results. On awakening from the trance, Lydia said each time she had visualized a scene with water and all the people, one by one, being forced into it to drown. She had felt herself being pulled down, followed by a blow. She would then scream, and the headache would follow.

Johnson called in another hypnotist for consultation. Dr. Murray (also a pseudonym) repeated the regression; but before the pain could intervene, he instructed her that she was ten years younger. At that moment it happened! Lydia started to talk, but not in sentences; rather, just an occasional phrase, partly in broken English, partly in a foreign language unknown to anyone present. Her voice became deep and masculine. Then from the mouth of the pretty thirty-seven-year-old woman came the chilling words: "I am a man! Jensen Jacoby!" (She pronounced it YEN'-SEN YAH'-KOBEE.)

Then she began in English, punctuated by foreign words, to describe a previous life. In this and the following sessions (tape recorded and monitored by Swedish linguists) she told Dr. Murray, in that low guttural voice, of living in a small village in Sweden about three centuries ago. (In the later sessions the subject spoke almost exclusively in Swedish, a language totally alien to Lydia. She was asked what she did for a living. "En Bond" [a farmer] was her answer.)

31

Jensen presented a simple personality compatible with the peasant life he detailed. He showed little knowledge of anything beyond his own small village and the trading center he visited on occasion. He raised cattle and horses and had built his own house made of stone. He and his wife Latvia had no children. With her eyes open, Lydia correctly identified objects such as a model of a 17th-century Swedish ship, which she correctly called "Skuta." She also recognized a wooden container used for measuring grain, a bow and arrow, and some poppy seeds. She identified and appeared to know how to use only simple tools.

After eight regressions, unexpectedly and without the aid of hypnosis, Jensen reappeared in Lydia. Dr. Johnson was able to dismiss him only after some effort. Due to the fear of permanent possession of his wife's person, Johnson ended the experiments, and no further attempts were made to communicate with Jensen. Although hypnosis was used in the — case of Lydia Johnson, Stevenson was still of the opinion that spontaneous utterances, particularly by children, are of even greater value. Stevenson has used hypnotism in a few cases, but states he has not succeeded even once in obtaining verifiable information on what seemed to be a previous life.

In summation, it should be stressed that Dr. Stevenson emphasized that his research had brought to light evidence *suggestive* of reincarnations, but not final proofs. When asked in an interview if he himself believed in reincarnation, he stated - in the spirit of true science — that he did not think his own belief of importance. What he did believe in is the truth of cases he investigated. Reincarnation, at least for him, was the best explanation he has been able to present.

Stevenson has noted that a rational man can sensibly believe in reincarnation on the basis of scientific evidence alone, although it appears that Dr. Stevenson, in spite of his remarkable contribution to the subject of reincarnation, did not experiment much with hypnosis in past-life regression. In addition, the cases he presents that lack such results from hypnotic past-life regression were most probably cases needing a specialized approach in order to elicit data.

It is important to carefully screen volunteers for hypnotic past-life regression. Their emotional status must be known. I personally eliminated cases from my own work that I suspected were pre-psychotic or in some way could become emotionally disturbed by the experience. On the other hand, I have found in my experience with nearly seven hundred cases, between 1979 and 1985, that stable people who undergo this kind of experience often raise their level of consciousness, understand themselves better, and are able to solve problems they could not before.

Any proof of reincarnation must begin with the telling of an account which is convincing to a scientific observer. The value of coincidence, for instance, lies in its accuracy. Anyone with inventive genius may weave together combinations of circumstances which would be very remarkable, if true. Perhaps the best piece of evidence of the truth of the following story is its simplicity. Another matter worth noting is the diary in which the record was made many years ago, and the fact that many of the people mentioned are still living to bear witness to its veracity.

This is the way one of the women told the story of her little half sister, younger by fifteen years:

> She was a queer mite from the beginning. She did not look like any member of the family. She was dark, while the rest of them all were fair, showing their Scottish-Irish ancestry unmistakably. As soon as she could talk in connected sentences she would tell herself fairy stories. She was her sister's special charge, her mother being a very busy woman. Besides her childish imagination there were bits of knowledge among them, that a baby could not possibly have absorbed in any way. Another unusual characteristic about her was that everything she did she seemed to do from habit, and in fact such was her insistence, although she was never able to explain what she meant by it. It was funny, this particularly embarrassed her mother and she reproved Anne repeatedly.
>
> The baby was a good little soul, and it seemed to try to obey. Then, in an absent-minded moment, it would introduce another after another occasion for mortification. When admonished by her mother for doing something

33

the wrong way, she would say she couldn't help it, and tears would come in her baby voice. She would say that she had always done it that way. So many were such small incidents of her habit of speech and thought and her tricks of manner and memory that they became a matter of fact.

One day, when she was four years old, she became very upset with her father about some matter. As she sat curled up on the floor, she announced her intention of leaving the family forever. With mock seriousness, her father told her not to go back to heaven. She said she did not come from heaven. She said this with firm assurance, to which the family had now become accustomed.

Continuing, she said she went first to the moon, which once had people on it. Her father continued to tease her about going to the moon. She told him that she had been there lots of times, sometimes as a man and sometimes as a woman. She spoke these things with such seriousness that her father laughed heartily, which enraged the child, for she intensely disliked being ridiculed.

She haughtily maintained that once she went to Canada as a man. She even remembered her name as that of Lishus Faber. When asked what she did for a living as Lishus Faber, she said she was a soldier. Once by chance, while reading a history of Canada, her sister read about the capture a little walled city by a company of soldiers. A young lieutenant with a small group of soldiers was responsible. His name was Aloysius LeFebre.[22]

A British psychiatrist, Arthur Guirdham, tells the following case of a woman patient which left him no other explanation but that of reincarnation. He first met "Mary" in 1961, when he was chief psychiatrist at Beth Hospital in England, where she consulted with him about persistent nightmares. These were accompanied by such loud screaming that she and her husband were afraid they would wake the neighbors.

Dr. Guirdham writes that Mary had been suffering since she was twelve from horrible dreams of murder and massacre. At first he suspected a neurosis, but could find none. Mary was a perfectly sane, ordinary housewife. Nothing wrong could be

34

discovered with her mental faculties. After a few months, she told him that when she was a girl, she used to write the dreams down. She had also written things that occurred spontaneously in her mind, things she couldn't determine about people and names of which she had never heard. She gave Dr. Guirdham the papers and he began to examine them. He was amazed to find that the verses of songs she had written as a school girl were in Medieval French, a subject of which she had no knowledge.

Guirdham sent a report of her story to Professor Pere Nellie of Toulouse University and asked his opinion. Nellie shortly wrote back that Mary had presented an accurate account of the Cathars, a group in Toulouse that subscribed to a Puritan philosophy during the thirteenth century.

Mary also described for Guirdham the massacre of the Cathars, and unveiled a horrid account of being burned at the stake. Dr. Guirdham was astounded. He had never really thought of reincarnation, never believed or disbelieved in it. Mary also told him that in her previous life she had been kept prisoner in a certain church crypt. Guirdham found that some religious prisoners were taken to such places when there was no room for them in regular prisons, and that some of them had indeed been kept in the crypt Mary mentioned.

In 1967, Guirdham decided to visit the south of France to investigate other of Mary's assertions. She gave him names and descriptions of people, places and events, all of which turned out to be accurate in great detail. He even found in the archives four of the signs she claimed to have written as a child. Word for word, they were as she claimed them to be.

In this account, Dr. Guirdham accumulated considerable evidence of the girl's knowledge of thirteenth-century life. Upon his request, she had made accurate drawings of old French coins, jewelry, the layout of buildings, and so forth. She was able to correctly identify persons whose authenticity was verified by an examination of records of the Inquisition.

As to her burning at the stake, the patient described the pain as being maddening, that one should pray to G-d when dying and in agony. She said that when you are burned to death you bleed. The blood dripped and hissed in the fire; she said she wished she had enough blood to put the flames out. The worst part was her eyes. She hated the thought of going blind. She tried to close her eyelids, but she couldn't. They must have been burned off, and now the flames were going to pluck her eyes out. Then the fire was over. She began to feel cold, icy cold. It occurred to her that she wasn't burning to death, but freezing to death. She was numb with the cold, and suddenly she began laughing. She had fooled those people who thought they could burn her. She thought she was a witch, she turned fire into ice.[23]

Another account of a verified past life has been related by motion picture actor Melvyn Douglas. Robin Hull was a small five-year-old boy who generally talked well for his age; but his mother would often notice him muttering strange sounds. One evening this performance was witnessed by a guest of Robin's parents, a woman who accepted reincarnation. She suggested introducing him to a professor she knew who was familiar with a number of Asiatic languages. Mrs. Hull agreed.

Several days later her friend came with the professor who listened carefully to this five-year-old boy and his strange jargon. The child was not at all self-conscious about these strange sounds he made. After more than an hour, the professor turned to Mrs. Hull and told her that the words Robin kept saying were from a dialect used in Northern Tibet.

The professor called Robin and asked him where he learned these words. Robin replied that he had learned them in school. (His mother at once pointed out that he had never been to school.) The boy explained this happened when he went to school — "before." The professor asked if Robin remembered what the school looked like. After a short deliberation, Robin said he remembered it was in the mountains, but they weren't the kind of mountains he and his family went to in the summer. The school was made of stone and the teachers were men. But they weren't dressed like the professor or dad; they had skirts with a sash around their waist that opened like a robe. Later, Robin gave a more detailed description of the school.

The professor was so impressed with everything Robin said that he undertook the long journey to Northern Tibet in search of the school. Eventually he found it in the KuenLun mountains, a rocky area, and not at all like the mountains where Robin spent his summers.

Rather than offering a "memory" of a former existence, the next episode from the life of a sixteen-year-old boy may possibly explain how (in this case the death of a boy at an early age) incarnation can occur quite soon.

In 1911, at the age of sixteen, I was staying about twelve miles away from my own home when a high wall was blown down by a sudden gust of wind as I was passing. A huge coping stone hit me on top of the head. It then seemed as if I could see myself lying on the ground, huddled up, with one corner of the stone resting on my head and quite a number of people rushing toward me. I watched them move the stone and someone took off his coat and put it under my head, and I heard all their comments: "Fetch a doctor." "His neck is broken." "Skull smashed."

One of the bystanders asked if anyone knew where I lived, and on being told I was lodging just around the corner, he instructed them to carry me there. All this time it appeared as though I were disembodied from the form lying on the ground and suspended in midair in the center of the group, but I could hear everything that was being said.

As they started to carry me it was remarked that my accident would come as a shock to my family, and I was immediately conscious of a desire to be with my mother. Instantly I saw myself at home as father and mother were just sitting down to their midday meal. On my entrance mother sat bolt upright in her chair and said, "Bert, something has happened to our boy."

There followed an argument, but my mother refused to be pacified and said that if she caught the 2 p.m. train she could be with me before 3 p.m. She had hardly left the room when there came a knock at the front door. It was a porter from the railway station with a telegram saying I was badly hurt.

Then suddenly I was again transported — this time it seemed to be against my wish — to a bedroom, where a woman I recognized was in bed and two other women were quietly bustling around, and a doctor was leaning

37

over the bed. Then the doctor had a baby in his hands. At once I became aware of an almost irresistible impulse to press my face through the back of the baby's head so that my face would come out at the same place as the child's.

The doctor said, "It looks as though we have lost them both." and again I felt the urge to take the baby's place to show him he was wrong, but the sight of my mother crying turned my thoughts to her direction, when straight-away I was in a railway carriage with her and my father.

I was still with them when they arrived at my lodgings and were shown the room where I had been put to bed. Mother sat beside the bed and I longed to comfort her, and the realization came that I ought to do the same thing I had felt impelled to do in the case of the baby and climb into the body on the bed. At last I succeeded, and the effort caused the real me to sit up in bed fully conscious. Mother made me lie down again, but I said I was all right, and remarked it was odd she knew something was wrong before the porter had brought the telegram.

Both she and Dad were amazed at my knowledge. Their astonishment was further increased when I repeated almost word for word some of the conversation they had at home and in the train. I said I had been close to birth as well as death, and told them that Mrs. Wilson, who lived close to us at home, had a baby that day, but it was dead because I would not get into its body. We subsequently learned that Mrs. Wilson died on the same day at 2:05 p.m. after delivering a stillborn girl.[24]

Thomas A. Edison had a strong interest in metaphysics and was an early and life-long member of the Theosophical Society. During his last illness, when reporters asked him if he believed in survival after death, he answered, The only survival I can conceive is to start a new earth cycle again." On his eightieth birthday, he was questioned as to whether he believed man had a soul. He replied that a man is composed of swarms of billions of highly-charged entities, which live in the cells. "I believe that when a man dies, this swarm deserts the body and goes out into space, but keeps on and enters another cycle of life, and is immortal.

"I cannot believe for a moment that life in the first instance originated in this insignificant little ball, which we call the earth ... The particles which combined to evolve living creatures on this planet of ours probably came from some other body elsewhere in the universe ... The more we learn the more we realize that there is life in the things which we used to regard as Inanimate, as lifeless . . .

"I don't believe for one moment that one life makes another life. Take our own bodies. I believe they are composed of myriads and myriads of infinitesimally small individuals, each in itself a unit of life, and these units work in squads - or swarms as I prefer to call them — and that these infinitesimally small units live forever. When we die these swarms of units, like swarms of bees, betake themselves elsewhere and go on functioning in some other form of environment."[25]

One evening in 1952, Ruth Simmons, a young housewife from Pueblo, Colorado, consented to be the subject of a hypnotic experiment. The hypnotist was a young businessman by the name of Morey Bernstein.

At first, she recalled some of the toys she loved when she was a year old. There was nothing unusual about this recollection. But in a second session Bernstein suggested she find herself in another place in another time. She was told to talk to him about it and answer his questions. She reported she was a little Irish girl named Bridey Murphy who lived in Cork with her mother, Kathleen, her barrister father, Duncan, and a brother. The year was 1806. She told how at fifteen she attended Mrs. Strayne's school in Cork where she learned to become a lady, and how later she married Brian McCarthy, and went to live in Belfast. Bridey's life story was pursued through the years up to her death at the age of sixty-six. She said that after her body's death, she existed in the spirit world for forty years, and then was reborn in Iowa in 1923, to take up her life as Ruth Simmons.

Checking later with the Irish Consulate, the British Information Service, the New York Public Library, and other informative sources, Bernstein found that many of Bridey's statements were consistent with historical facts. Ruth had never visited Ireland and had no normal way of knowing the facts she revealed under hypnosis. Skeptics stated that the hypnotized girl may have brought forth these facts from a memory bank of things she had read or otherwise observed, events that could have been woven into the tale of Bridey. It was also assumed that this young woman might have gained her knowledge through telepathy or clairvoyance. Also, it was considered important to know what happened in the conversations that took place with the girl when awake, as well as when hypnotized.[26]

In her book *Reliving Past Lives: The Evidence Under Hypnosis,* Dr. Helen Wambach wrote about her research into the lives of 1,100 volunteers. Her findings were impressive. Dr. Wambach first regressed certain groups to the time periods of 1850, 1700, 1500, and 25 B.C. and 500 B.C. In following sessions, she regressed the same group to various time periods ranging from 2000 B.C. and 1000 B.C. to A.D. 400, 800 and 1200. Next, she suggested her subjects recall a vacation they had taken in the past five years, and to vividly recall where they had slept on the trip, and the scenery and the people they saw. She then suggested that they "fly" to the sky, rest on a fluffy white cloud, and then float around the world and pick a place among the ones that would be called out. She asked them to choose a place to experience a past life, where the images were most vivid, a place toward which they felt emotionally drawn. These instructions resulted in the most vivid experiences of all.

The fourth session had to do with the state between lives, between the death of the physical body and the current incarnation. To get this information, Dr. Wambach needed to take them to a deep level.

Next, Dr. Wambach started evaluating the statistical information on classes, sex, geographical location, and other variables. To her surprise, she found only eleven data sheets out of 1,088 with clear evidence of a discrepancy. An important finding was that the subjects shared equally both male and female lives in the past. This was considered quite remarkable, since most of Dr. Warnbach's volunteers were females. She pointed out that evidence gathered from a random sampling of the general population (when asked if they were to be born again, would they prefer to be male or female) the percentage of people that chose to be males was much higher than 50 % of the population. This appears to cast a new light on her findings on regression under hypnosis, where she discovered the equality between the sexes — indicating that we do not always get what we ask for!

The steady increase in population is explained by Dr. Wambach simply that more souls choose to incarnate on Earth as conditions here are more attractive; here people have the opportunity to experience - to live out - the purposes they have created for themselves.

Dr. Wambach regressed some 750 people. Through her they relived extraordinary moments, days and months before they actually emerged into the world. One of the questions she asked them was whether a person *chooses* to be born. This was usually answered affirmatively (though they were sometimes advised by those on "the other side" to make the choice.

Another question she posed was: why choose the twentieth century? Although answers varied, most people emphasized that greater learning was possible in this time of change; others expressed a wish to repair a relationship they had not worked out in a past life.

Another question she asked was whether one chose one's own sex for the next incarnation. The answer was often that this had to do with the degree or completion of one's experiences on the Earth plane. Does a person know who is one's mother by a previous birth? Yes, most of the time, was the answer. In this connection, many of the volunteers reported that they met a number of different people from previous lives in their present existence in order to complete an unworked relationship - or because of a certain attraction. Another interesting question was whether an individual was incarnated in the fetus prior to birth. Although varied, the major response was that only at the time of birth did the soul enter and stabilize itself in the body; during pregnancy it would often enter and re-enter intermittently.[27]

Are the poets correct in their claim of love's immortality? Some researchers into past lives would have us think so. One psychic researcher, using regressive hypnosis, returned people to their past lives to prove that they lived together in earlier lifetimes. Many of those regressed had been attracted to each

41

other for several lives, both for good and bad. In many cases they had not learned their lessons in previous bitter experiences, and so they had to be reborn together to correct their "errors."[28]

In *Life After Life*, Raymond Moody also presents case histories that support a belief in life after death. His work was an astounding best seller. It presented experiences of persons, though declared clinically dead, yet whose descriptions are so similar, vivid and overwhelmingly positive that they offer dramatic evidence to support a theory of reincarnation. In his case histories Moody gives accounts of patients who, during their clinical death, would leave their body, watch and hear what was occurring. After resuscitation, they would give an account, detail by detail, of who helped them be restored to life, what kind of medication was used, and other particulars. They claimed they left their physical body, hovered at the ceiling, and observed all these details.[29]

One example of such a past life is that of actor Glenn Ford. Under hypnosis Ford spoke French with an accent prevalent during the period in which he lived. He later discovered five of his past lives.

Of particular significance is the fact that knowledge of previous existences learned through hypnosis or other means permits people to permanently change their present lives — usually for the better. Many discover in themselves innate abilities that can only be explained by past-life experiences.

One such case is that of Mrs. Delores Jay, 57, the wife of the Reverend Carroll E. Jay, pastor of the Anerson Memorial United Methodist Church in Gretna, Virginia. Mrs. Jay could recall a past life in Germany and spoke German under hypnosis - a language of which she had no prior knowledge, nor had she ever been to Germany, nor had the opportunity of learning what life was like there a century earlier.

In 1981, I was asked to become part of an investigation into a case of reincarnation conducted by H. N. Banerjee, research director of the Center for Para-analytical Studies in San Diego, California. Dr. Banerjee is also author of *Americans Who Have Been Reincarnated*.

The case involved a three-year-old girl from Des Moines, Iowa who was raised in a Catholic family, where no word of' reincarnation was mentioned. She said that in a past life she was a person named Joe Wilke, who had died in a motorcycle accident on July 20, 1975 in Brookfield, Illinois, a suburb of Chicago. Joe Wilke's wife, Sheila, also perished in the same accident.

Officer T. Michowski of the Brookfield Police Department and the County Morgue confirmed the deaths. Following is an excerpt from a letter I sent Dr. Banerjee:

August 6, 1981

Dear Dr. Banerjee:

After extensive checking and research, I have come up with the following information for you about the people you asked me to check on:

Joseph Wilke was born on April 14, 1937 in Iowa. He lived in Brookfield, Illinois at 8871 Plainfield Road, and was married to Shelia Wilke, with two children, a result of this union. The daughter was sixteen and the son eleven at the time of their parents' death. He was a member of his son's little league team. Brookfield police have a record of a Honda motorcycle registered to a J. Wilke in 1975. He died on July 20, 1975 of multiple injuries and severe trauma at 5:33 p.m. The accident occurred on Interstate 55 and Wolf Road in Indian Head Park, Illinois, at 4:55 p.m.

Sheila Wilke was born on August 10, 1939 in Illinois. The time of her death was 5:34 p.m. on July 20, 1975 of multiple injuries sustained in the accident.

Sincerely,

43

CHAPTER FOUR
Astrology and Reincarnation

Hippocrates, the father of medicine, said "A physician without a knowledge of astrology has no right to call himself a physician." In fifth-century Greece, it was common knowledge that the stars influence the destiny of man; by the same token, different illnesses can be explained according to different planetary positions. As a+ consequence, a science within a science evolved. Physicians treated their patients with considerable attention to their zodiacal sign and other influences indicated by their astrological chart.

As a psychiatrist I was at first skeptical of astrology. Having been "programmed" to regard this area with doubt — based on a so-called "scientific attitude" — I failed to carefully and scientifically observe what astrology really signified and what its impact would be on my practice. After several personal experiences were confirmed by astrology, I decided to find out if such discoveries could find application among my patients. Obviously, my diagnosis and treatment had nothing to do with astrology. My working astrology was done merely for my own curiosity, to observe if my psychiatric assessment of a patient would, to some extent, agree with the characteristics of his or her zodiacal sign.

To my surprise, I found that 80 percent or more of what I discovered just by a birthdate helped me in assessing a patient; and it quite accurately matched my psychiatric assessment of that individual. I doubted, however, that any one of my colleagues would be inclined to follow in my footsteps, and I continued my inquiry into this phenomenon somewhat secretly. I must insist, however, that astrology does not comprise my general approach to psychiatric treatment.

When one comes to the subject of reincarnation and karma, it is impossible not to look carefully at the concept of celestial influence on the subconscious. This influence appears to greatly contribute to an individual's personality and would explain previous life experiences, as well as current ones. With this in mind, I gradually became more absorbed in searching out the validity of astrological concepts and possible ways they might explain reincarnation.

I was especially impressed by Jeanne Dixon's work, *Yesterday, Today and Forever,* in which she shows how astrology can assist one in finding a place in G-d's master plan. She questions whether it is chance or G-d's plan that the twelve apostles correspond to the twelve signs of the Zodiac. She asks whether astrology and religion are opposing beliefs — or can an understanding of one's astrological strengths and weaknesses lead to a richer life and more profound commitment to faith.

Astrology is an important and valuable tool to help people to know themselves. When a person applies the correct knowledge, he becomes more conscious of the influences of the cosmos upon his subconscious, and thereby is in a better position to modify negative influences and accentuate positive ones.

Since ancient times astrology has influenced the practice of medicine and assisted in recommending remedies for various illnesses such as headache, kidney, heart problems, gout, and so forth.

In 1968, the Czech government founded the Astra Research Center for Planned Parenthood, which offers astrological advice, based upon the position of the planets. The foundation claims to offer safe and reliable birth control without pills, contraceptives or operations, to help many sterile women become fertile and when they do, help them deliver healthy babies.

Scientists from centuries past — from Hippocrates to Kepler and Leibnez — have practiced astrology. Ancient astrologers have always maintained that fertility periods are bonded to the waxing and waning of the moon. A Czech psychiatrist, Dr. Eugen Jonas, discovered a planetary configuration that provides a key to understanding the relationship of the sun and the moon at each woman's birth. He has shown how one can determine with near precision the date when a woman will become pregnant, as well as on what day conception should take place in order to deliver a girl or boy.

Whether we realize it or not, our lives are ordered by the planets and their heavenly movements. A growing number of people are coming to accept this fact, judging from the wide interest in astrology today. It should be emphasized, however, that the planets influence our subconscious only. Through our will power, the conscious mind can change any unfavorable predicament. Such ideas seem to find a readier acceptance behind the Iron Curtain than in the West.

Since Carl Jung first encouraged the study of astrology, there has been an awakening of interest among certain scientists and psychologists, even if at first such interest has arisen through a desire to prove it all a part of nonsense. On the other hand, there is now developing an increasing appreciation of the value of astrology in psychological counseling; a birth chart gives the counselor a most helpful tool in developing insight into his patient's problems. Such knowledge can be of immense value to doctors, psychotherapists, personal managers and career advisors; and it is hoped that the future will witness the exact time of birth recorded on all birth certificates, so that one's astrological past and future can be studied. The birth one chart is undoubtedly a blueprint for the life experience of any person. The wonderful exactitude of heavenly order and the miraculous outcome to be recognized in every aspect of nature forces thinking persons to conclude that there must be a good, wise and constructive reason for human pain and suffering. This reason can be discovered by a study of esoteric astrology, which demonstrates the working out of a deep spiritual law, as indicated by the planets and constellations.

Esoteric astrology is based on the law of reincarnation, the fact that this present life span is not unique, but part of a long cycle of experience which stretches far back into the past and, even today, prepares itself for the future. Numerous times are we born into a new physical body, and we experience the joys, sorrows, the struggles, the failures and the successes of life. We are not on this journey alone. According to those teachers who possess knowledge of spiritual law, we journey in groups. We reincarnate with those we have loved, those we have hated, those who have helped us, those with whom we have suffered. We may find ourselves in different or even alternating relationships — at times as master or as servant, at times as parent or as child, or as husband, or wife.

All of these experiences help us to understand precisely how another individual feels in any situation, to feel with him until

47

slowly we learn in detail how to treat another as we ourselves would like to be treated in the same circumstances. To a considerable extent, these lessons are in accord with the law of cause and effect, known in the Eastern religions as *karma*. This universal law works in parallel with that of reincarnation and ensures that we are born into the correct situations and with the proper group of individuals to balance our debts for past errors and wrong doing — or as a reward for "good acts."

We are born with various talents which in some circumstances need almost no training to turn into superior skills. Such remarkable gifts are the result of hard work and perseverance put into previous lives, for nothing is ever forgotten. Also, we may be born with disabilities or limitations which will compel us to develop skills of a nature other than what we would really like.

In many ways life on earth is a schooling ground. We reincarnate again into the classroom of earthly life with a certain program of instruction, according to our birth chart. The subjects properly mastered in previous lives will come easily, and those which we failed will have to be repeated until properly learned. Along with reincarnation and karma, two other laws are operative — the law of opportunity and the law of balance. The law of opportunity makes sure that within every experience of the soul exists a marvelous opportunity to raise our consciousness by acquiring a skill or "stronghold," a power of endurance which will help us in the future, as well as providing us with a unique opportunity to serve others. Edgar Cayce described this law as "the law of grace." Joan Hodgson observes, "it is that divine blessing, that inner contentment and peace which arise in the soul as it patiently struggles to pay back its karmic debts in the environment in which it Is put with cheerfulness, courage and kindness.

"The law of balance seems to be as fundamental in the soul life as it is in the physical world, where it manifests in the swing of the tides, alternating heat and cold, light and darkness, positive and negative electric currents, acid and alkaline chemical balance, and in many other ways. One way in which it manifests itself on the soul plane is to cause the soul to incarnate sometimes in a male, sometimes in a female body. This of course gives valuable opportunities for working out karmic debts incurred at both the emotional and the physical level through sex life."[30] Alternating experiences of wealth and poverty, success and failure, dominance and submission as well as experiences of an extrovert or introvert temperament gradually bring the soul to complete self-mastery. At the end of each incarnation the soul withdraws from the physical body, which is relinquished like an outer garment, and enters an inner world just as real as the physical, although it is invisible to ordinary sight.

What follows is a time of rest and refreshment, a holiday from the school of earthly learning. Next comes a period when the soul is gently and gradually led to a deeper understanding of the mystery of its own being, and led to a reassessment of its progress in the unfolding of its G-dlike powers. The soul is presented with a full picture of its numerous incarnations on earth. Gradually it begins to grasp a vision of those gifts of the spirit which, when developed to perfection, will enable it to make its own contribution to the joy and peace of the whole. It realizes that only further learning experiences in a physical body will develop these gifts; thus it senses the need to return once more to an earth incarnation.

It is difficult to assess the span of years that separates one life from another. Sometimes the soul will spend a considerable time resting in the heavenly world; on the other hand, the spiritual evolution of races reaching its peak of reincarnation is speeded up, especially with the more evolved souls eager to come back to help the masses rise from darkness and suffering.

Sometimes hundreds of years lapse between reincarnations, at other times only a century or less. It is known that in certain circumstances a child will come back almost immediately — often to the same family. In short, no specific rule seems to govern the time between incarnations.

A question often asked is "Why can't we recall our past lives?" If you stop to reflect on the difficulty with which we remember even the details of childhood or events occurring only a few years back, you can readily appreciate how impossible it is to recall happenings of a century ago, perhaps many thousands of years ago, by means of a physical brain that is without any impressions of those occurrences. However, as one proceeds along the path of unfolding, the conscious mind becomes more and more sensitive to the vibrations of past experiences; but these vibrations create images in the mind of scenes in one's past, and so gradually the memory of past experiences and reincarnations becomes clearer.

Many people suffer at the thought of not finding their loved ones when they return to the earth plane from the other side. They also fear that when they come to the spirit world they will find their friends reincarnated. It does not seem to work this way. We move up the evolutionary path in groups and in families. "The whole purpose of spiritual evolution," writes Hodgson. "is for love to reign supreme and for all negative vibrations to be eventually absorbed into the positive good — which is all love, all wisdom, all power."

This means reaching the great white Light, the eternal Light in the heavens, as stated in Eastern esoteric teachings. G-d said, Let there be Light, and there was Light. All creation came from that Light. These teachings are based on the understanding that from that Light we have come and to that Light we return. Our souls beam that Light, and in their experience, acquire wisdom, love and strength, having developed at the end of that journey into being the perfect son/daughter of G-d.

According to reincarnational astrological data, each sun sign of the Zodiac represents a certain element: fire, earth, water or air. Accordingly, one has to learn certain general lessons in his or her current lifetime. Aries, Leo and Sagittarius, the fire signs, have to learn the lesson of love. The earth signs — Taurus, Virgo and Capricorn — are to learn the lesson of service. The water signs — Cancer, Scorpio, and Pisces — must learn the lesson of peace. Gemini, Libra and Aquarius, the air signs, have to master the lesson of brotherhood. People born between the nineteenth and twenty-fourth of any month are in a transitional state of development in their earthly experience. Their period of apprenticeship under their existing sign is almost over for the time being; they are approaching their new sign in order that their experiences of life will to some extent be the blending of the lessons of two signs.

The doctrine of karma, though originating in the East, has become increasingly better known and appreciated by the Western world during the past several decades. Everything in the universe is brought under the influence of karma, the law of cause and effect. Nothing escapes it. Through the study of astrology we can gain a better understanding of karma and the kind of experiences one can expect during our lifetime — and, more importantly, how the mistakes of previous lives can be corrected. This can be learned just by knowing the time of our birth. More specifically, by studying the South Moon's node we learn those aspects of our character brought from previous lives. We do this by developing the traits of the North Moon's node.

The South Node is symbolic of man's past. It does not necessarily symbolize only one past incarnation, but rather a combination of thoughts, ideas, attitudes and happenings from each incarnation whose accumulated and unresolved effects brought about the creation of the present life patterns. Therefore, the South Moon's Node may represent hundreds and thousands of previous lives; as a mathematical average would correspond to one of the twelve signs of the Zodiac.

The South Moon's Node should not be confused with the sun sign of the individual. The sun sign indicates the planetary position as related to the sun during the time of birth. It is one of the twelve positions or signs, and has its respective name, i.e., Taurus, Libra, etc. For example, the sun sign Taurus, and its respective divisions, generally give the individual his personality traits in this lifetime; but it does not necessarily indicate where he came from in terms of past lives experiences, nor where he is going. Thus, not much can be interpreted from the sun sign and its respective division concerning the learning purpose in the current life. The South Moon's Node throws light upon the individual's past life experiences.

The North Moon's Node comes to guide the current life in order to overcome negative karmic effects. The South Moon's Node means the time prior to an individual's last birth, when the moon was positioned in the southern hemisphere, and in a specific zodiacal sign according to the position of other planets as they related to the moon. As stated earlier, the South Moon's Node sign must not necessarily be the same as the sun sign. If you take the sun sign of Taurus, as an example, its corresponding South Moon's Node does not have to be necessarily Taurus, but may be Virgo, Aquarius, etc., according to past life experiences of the individual.

The North Moon's Node means the first time, immediately after an individual's birth, that the moon crossed the line into the northern hemisphere of the earth. The North Moon's Node sign would be one of the twelve zodiacal signs, determined by the position of the planets and their relationship to the moon in the northern hemisphere of the earth. The South and the North Nodes of the moon, as well as the astrological signs in which they are placed, are directly opposite from one another, which is a logical way of karmically balancing each other.[31]

In my current study I found out that a majority of my past life regression subjects related former life birthdates, within the past 200 years, that correspond to their birthdates in this lifetime. In both lifetimes, the past one and the current one, these dates coincide with the same North or South Node positions.

This statistical finding (two odds in twelve) suggests a plausible continuity between the two lifetimes, which are in temporal proximity to each other.

For example, a subject eight years old, born July 22, 1972 (which corresponds to a Capricorn North Mood Node), under a past life regression, reported being born on January 30, 1862 — which also corresponds to a Capricorn North Moon Node.

The following is a chart with the mathematically calculated Moon's North Node positions from 1850 to 1999:

THE MOON'S NORTH NODE POSITIONS
1850-1899

January 1, 1850 - May 10, 1851	Leo
May 11, 1851 - November 25, 1852	Cancer
November 26, 1852 - June 16, 1854	Gemini
June 17, 1854 - January 3, 1856	Taurus
January 4, 1856 - July 23, 1857	Aries
July 24, 1857 - February 9, 1859	Pisces
February 10, 1859 - August 29, 1860	Aquarius
August 30, 1860 - March 18, 1862	Capricorn
March 19, 1862 - October 6, 1863	Sagittarius
October 7, 1863 - April 25, 1865	Scorpio
April 26, 1865 - November 12, 1866	Libra
November 13, 1866 - June 1. 1868	Virgo

June 2, 1868 - December 20, 1869	Leo
December 21. 1869 - July 9, 1871	Cancer
July 10, 1871 - January 25, 1873	Gemini
January 26, 1873 - August 15, 1874	Taurus
August 16, 1874 - March 3, 1876	Aries
March 4, 1876 - September 21, 1877	Pisces
September 22, 1877 - April 10, 1879	Aquarius
April 11, 1879 - October 28, 1880	Capricorn
October 29, 1880 - May 17, 1882	Sagittarius
May 18, 1882 - December 5, 1883	Scorpio
December 6, 1883 - June 24, 1885	Libra
June 25, 1885 - January 12, 1887	Virgo
January 13, 1887 - July 31, 1888	Leo
August 1, 1888 - February 17, 1890	Cancer
February 18, 1890 - September 7, 1891	Gemini
September 8, 1891 - March 26, 1893	Taurus
March 27, 1893 - October 13, 1894	Aries
October 14, 1894 - May 2, 1896	Pisces
May 3, 1896 - November 20, 1897	Aquarius
November 21, 1897 - June 9, 1899	Capricorn
June 10, 1899 - December 31, 1899	Sagittarius

1900 - 1949

January 1, 1900 - December 28, 1900	Sagittarius
December 29, 1900 - July 17. 1902	Scorpio
July 18, 1902 - February 4, 1904	Libra
February 5, 1904 - August 23, 1905	Virgo
August 24, 1905 - March 13, 1907	Leo
March 14, 1907 - September 29, 1908	Cancer
September 30, 1908 - April 18, 1910	Gemini
April 19, 1910 - November 7, 1911	Taurus
November 8, 1911 - May 26, 1913	Aries
May 27, 1913 - December 13, 1914	Pisces
December 14, 1914 - July 2, 1916	Aquarius
July 3, 1916 - January 19, 1918	Capricorn
January 20, 1918 - August 9, 1919	Sagittarius
August 10, 1919 - February 26, 1921	Scorpio
February 27, 1921 - September 15, 1922	Libra
September 16, 1922 - April 4, 1924	Virgo

April 5, 1924 - October 22, 1925	Leo
October 23, 1925 - May 12, 1927	Cancer
May 13, 1927 - November 28, 1928	Gemini
November 29, 1928 - June 18, 1930	Taurus
June 19, 1930 - January 6, 1932	Aries
January 7, 1932 - July 25, 1933	Pisces
July 26, 1933 - February 12, 1935	Aquarius
February 13, 1935 - September 1, 1936	Capricorn
September 2, 1936 - March 21, 1938	Sagittarius
March 22, 1938 - October 9, 1939	Scorpio
October 10, 1939 - April 27, 1941	Libra
April 28, 1941 - November 15, 1942	Virgo
November 16, 1942 - June 3, 1944	Leo
June 4, 1944 - December 23, 1945	Cancer
December 24, 1945 - July 11, 1947	Gemini
July 12, 1947 - January 28, 1949	Taurus
January 29, 1949 - December 31, 1949	Aries

1950 - 1999

January 1, 1950 - August 17, 1950	Aries
August 18, 1950 - March 7, 1952	Pisces
March 8, 1952 - October 2, 1953	Aquarius
October 3, 1953 - April 12, 1955	Capricorn
April 13, 1955 - November 4, 1956	Sagittarius
November 5, 1956 - May 21, 1958	Scorpio
May 22, 1958 - December 8, 1959	Libra
December 9, 1959 - July 3, 1961	Virgo
July 4, 1961 - January 13, 1963	Leo
January 14, 1963 - August 5, 1964	Cancer
August 6, 1964 - February 21, 1966	Gemini
February 22, 1966 - September 10, 1967	Taurus
September 11, 1967 - April 3, 1969	Aries
April 4, 1969 - October 15, 1970	Pisces
October 16, 1970 - May 5, 1972	Aquarius
May 6, 1972 - November 22, 1973	Capricorn
November 23, 1973 - June 12, 1975	Sagittarius
June 13, 1975 - December 29, 1976	Scorpio
December 30, 1976 - July 19, 1978	Libra
July 20, 1978 - February 5, 1980	Virgo

February 6, 1980 - August 25, 1981	Leo
August 26, 1981 - March 14, 1983	Cancer
March 15, 1983 - October 1, 1984	Gemini
October 2, 1984 - April 20, 1986	Taurus
April 21, 1986 - November 8, 1987	Aries
November 9, 1987 - May 28, 1989	Pisces
May 29, 1989 - December 15, 1990	Aquarius
December 16, 1990 - July 4, 1992	Capricorn
July 5, 1992 - January 21, 1994	Sagittarius
January 22, 1994 - August 11, 1995	Scorpio
August 12, 1995 - February 27, 1997	Libra
February 28, 1997 - September 17, 1998	Virgo
September 18, 1998 - December 31, 1999	Leo

CHAPTER FIVE
Using Guided Imagery and Hypnosis
in Past Life Regression

In the beginning I decided to use a method that would be based mainly on guided imagery. In this method, the volunteer is guided by myself into regression from the current lifetime. According to the degree of the volunteer's suggestibility, I use different modifications of this technique. I also discuss with the subjects the various theories regarding reincarnation and, to my surprise, I have found that nearly half of the volunteers believed openly in it! I also briefly acquaint each subject with hypnosis, define it as a state of altered consciousness in which an individual experiences a state between sleep and wakefulness. Though an individual may easily fall asleep in that state, I emphasize that remaining receptive to my suggestions is essential (I caution against falling asleep!).

I find that in my experience about 40 percent of those hypnotized will reach a deep trance. This state often produces in the individual a dream-like feeling, and with it "a dream" which can or can not be remembered. Usually, recall is scarce. The trance — both superficial and medium, creates a relaxed state in which one experiences a feeling of floating or the like, and a sense of timelessness. In a superficial trance, which is quite close to wakefulness, there is a good possibility of "tuning in" to tile subconscious mind. About 30 percent of those I have worked with reach that state; the medium trance is reached by roughly another 30 percent, and can be defined as a state in between the two described. Approximately 90 to 95 percent of those who volunteer for past life regression can be hypnotized under tile above definition, and about 90 percent of the ones who are hypnotized experience a so-called past life. Questions regarding hypnosis are answered prior to the experiment.

One of the questions that comes up often from my patients is clearly understandable: "Am I going to lose control of or have my will power weakened by hypnosis?" The answer is a resounding no. In any ethical type of hypnosis, the purpose is to assist the individual in a positive direction rather than weaken his will power. A person has full authority to veto any suggestion that seems inadequate.

Another question frequently raised is: "What happens if I don't wake up?" In my 31 years of experience with hypnosis, it has happened only a few times that a person found it difficult to recover from a trance state. When I would ask such a person why he or she did not come out more quickly from the trance, the answer would almost always be unanimous, "I enjoyed it so much that I hated to snap out of it. Other questions people ask pertain to methods of treatment. "Do suggestions given under hypnosis last?" Yes, if you work at it, it will work for you.

I stress that the hypnotic experience may be regarded as treatment. There are two factors that make the difference between failure and success — self-help and a positive mental attitude. If both are applied there is no doubt that help will come as a cure or considerable improvement in this condition.

Another question raised is whether there is any danger involved in being hypnotized. I know of no danger in the practice of hypnosis or self-hypnosis, so long as the person so subjected is not initially dangerous to himself or others. If anything, hypnosis may uncover an already existing potential for violence. However, it has been my experience that such a possibility is practically nonexistent. Volunteers and patients should always be screened before hypnosis is undertaken.

Finally, many people are apprehensive about unpleasant experiences during regression. I assure them that I help them avoid negative feelings and pain. Eventually. I ask them to become neutral observers and report to me what they see, hear, or experience as a detached observer, as it were. One qualification that seems essential is making the volunteers generally understand how their minds work. I explain how the conscious and the subconscious interact, how the subconscious will be the retriever of possible past lives; but because their subconscious expresses itself through illogical, symbolical or pictorial language, it will often not make sense to the conscious mind, which operates in logical concepts. It may not grasp nor accept the productions of the subconscious.

If one is not aware of this "language" difference, any dream-like material that does not make sense to the conscious mind will not be accepted by it. Therefore, the conscious mind is to remain still — observing, understanding, and accepting the language of the subconscious. Eventually, the subject undertakes the journey of regression and the subconscious reveals the data on names, dates, geographical locations, and so forth, which are to be held up for later verification.

One of the difficulties of this research consists in the fact that the subconscious does not lie. Rather, it often disguises information, especially names and numbers, making such information very difficult — if not impossible — to verify.

Initially, I hypnotized about four hundred subjects. I did so without thought of any scientific study; the motivation was simple curiosity. Later I decided regression into the ancient past seemed inconclusive and nonscientific — even for the satisfaction of my curiosity, since I could verify nothing through official documents. Gradually I restricted my research to the investigation of previous lives that took place one to two hundred years prior to the subject's birthdate in this lifetime. I now stood on sounder scientific ground.

At first I hoped to find a reasonably high correlation among my volunteers in their geographical, social, and historical descriptions. This proved to be an immense work, however, involving large groups of subjects, perhaps thousands, and I was forced to dismiss its possibility. Although my methods varied during the years, I have lately found a modified inductive method that has been quite successful. It includes to a certain extent Helen Wambach's approach.[27] Essentially, I resort to the standard hypnotic procedures to bring about relaxation. I then turn their attention backwards in time. A typical procedure might continue thus: Find a picture of yourself between the ages of thirteen and eighteen. Look closely at that picture, see what you are wearing in the picture. Tell me if you like what you are wearing. How does it feel on your skin? What shoes do you wear?

"I want you to go back even further into your memory and find a picture of yourself between the ages of six and twelve. Where were you when this picture was taken? Now you are in the third grade, sitting in your regular seat. Where is the window? On your right, left, behind you? The teacher is in front of the class. Is the teacher a man or a woman?

"Now I want you to go back in time and find a photo of yourself between the ages of one and five. Look into the eyes of that child. Do you remember being in such a small body? Imagine you are three years old and sitting in the bathtub. Look down at your thighs, your knees, your ankles, your toes. How does it feel being in this small a body? Become vividly aware of your body as a three-year-old. Now I want you to line up all three pictures or images of yourself, as a young child, in middle childhood, as an adolescent and add to them your present image. What is it that has remained the same? Your body has changed, hasn't it, as old cells have died and new ones developed. Your clothes have changed, the background of the pictures have changed. What is it that continues to be you? I want you to be aware that each of the snapshots represents only one-twentieth of a second of the time you have been alive in this lifetime.

"Behind the picture of yourself as a young child imagine a row of snapshots of the other one-twentieths of a second that you lived through. See, the row stretches into infinity! Behind that picture of yourself in middle-childhood stretches the other one-twentieth of a second to infinity. Behind the picture of yourself as an adolescent stretches the row of the other one-twentieths of a second that you lived through in that period of your life. Behind your present image stretches the row of the other one-twentieth of a second that you have lived up to now.

"If all the changes in your body and your feelings about yourself, your ambitions, your dreams, had been caught by a camera, they too would stretch to infinity. Look back now on these endless rows of snapshots that represent your past! How much of it do you recall? Almost all of it is lost to your conscious mind. The past you think you remember is a story told to you by your conscious mind, which picks up bits and pieces of memories from the memory bank of your subconscious, and puts them together to make a story called 'My Past,' much as a film editor strings together snippets from exposed film to make a movie. The past you think you remember is fragmentary and limited. For every moment in your past that you thought you hated someone, there is a moment when you loved a person. For every moment in your past when you felt guilty and ashamed, there is a moment when you felt triumphant and quietly satisfied. Lost in those endless rows of pictures of your growing-up years are the potentials you have never developed; feelings you have long since forgotten; opportunities you have never realized.

"I want you to recognize now that your past is as changeable as your future. You may choose to realize aspects of your past life long since forgotten, and now put them to positive, constructive, and healthy use. This is what is called free will."

CHAPTER SIX
Cases of Past Life Regressions

The following cases of past life regression represent some of the most interesting examples from my files. All sessions were recorded on tape.

Perhaps the most amazing case I have yet encountered is that of Doris G., a 22-year-old woman who first came to me seeking help for depression through hypnotherapy. Despite a number of treatments, she failed to get better. Eventually, she became suicidal and was hospitalized. After several months Doris improved enough to be released, but her depression continued. She suffered from a depression that did not respond to either psychotherapy or anti-depressive drugs. Eventually her suicidal tendencies lessened and she became functional enough to be discharged. However, her functioning was still marginal. She found it difficult to maintain a job, relate to her family, either live by herself or live with friends. In short, she experienced a great deal of hardship in her relationships.

I asked Doris if she would submit to a past life regression, and she agreed — though she could not always enter a deep trance when hypnotized. She appeared to have difficulty in maintaining her attention sufficiently to focus on my suggestions. The first time that she volunteered, she was quite afraid. In spite of my determined attempts to hypnotize and regress her, everything proved futile. But I continued to encourage her, explaining that in the beginning the subconscious may be quite unwilling until it gets used to the idea, and feels safe enough to permit the experience to happen.

Eventually I hypnotized her. Initially, she reached only superficial trance, but during the course of regression it gradually deepened, and she was able to offer the following information:

She once lived in Cornwall, a town in Orange County, New York, during the early 1800's. Her name was Lisa Arthur, and she was eight years old. She mentioned that she was a student in the third grade, in the Middletown School, which was a female boarding school, a private school, in Middletown, New

York, some distance from Cornwall. She gave the teacher's name, Mrs. Pfeiffer. Her father took Lisa there by carriage. Lisa could describe Cornwall, and the house. She described the grass, the trees, and the Hudson River, also a town nearby that could be a town close to their house. The house was gray, with some pink and black colors. The rooftop was black. She was living on a farm, and this was a farmhouse. Also she could see in her visual field other farmhouses.

She described the people in the household, her grandfather, Samuel Arthur, 58 years old, a farmer; John, her father, 35, a farmer; Sara or Elaine, 29, her mother, a housewife; Tom, a six-year-old brother; Mary, her grandmother, deceased when Lisa was four, and was buried by the house; the grave was marked by a cross. Lisa thought she also had an older sister, and two sisters who probably died before Lisa was eight — Mary, three, and Alice, eight months old. She used to go to church, a Catholic Church, located in Cornwall; the name of the church was St. Theresa. Lisa claimed she was baptized there. There was a store in Cornwall, the Merchant's Store, and there was an older salesman there. Lisa died on April 18, 1812 at the age of 12, she committed suicide. She jumped from the fourth floor. through a window, as she was unhappy with her life. It seems that she was alone and was spending a great deal of time away from her family in the private school in Middletown. Lisa claims that after her death, there was an announcement in the newspaper that she fell from a window and could not be saved, as she subsequently died due to a head injury. She was buried near her grandmother's grave, close to the house. On the grave headstone is an inscription: "Lisa Arthur, 1812." She mentioned no karmic connection. Lisa reported another lifetime where she died in Blarney, Ireland after she committed suicide as a teenager, by banging her head on the walls of a room to which she was confined by her family.

The interesting therapeutic result of these past life regressions was that Doris started functioning better, and integrating better the knowledge of her conscious discovery of herself. The idea of suicide became futile, since it had not solved anything in past lives, and the problem continued in her current life. As a consequence, she has been gradually improving in her mental status and outlook on life, and had completely relinquished the idea of suicide.

The remarkable results through investigation, by myself and a genealogist, Nancy Fredericks, led to establishing that Lisa gave accurate information with regard to the town where she was born, Cornwall. In the census of the population of 1810, the name Samuel Arthur appears as the only Samuel Arthur in that census for Orange County. Also, it is clear that Samuel Arthur was the head of the family, and a miller, as documents state him to be a witness in court at one time regarding an inheritance. Also, John was the father, and the people in the household were basically a younger brother 6 years old; apparently there was a female who fits the mother's age. Also, there was an older sister that appears there. The two younger sisters were probably deceased. Another interesting finding was that Lisa was the only girl between the ages of 10 and 16 at the time of the census. (See figure no. 1) She described quite well the location of her house, the farm and the pond that can only be Arthur Pond. At one time she described the Hudson River, and this could be seen by her only in Cornwall, and not in Middletown. Middletown is quite far from her home, and her father used to take her by carriage to her school. The name of the teacher, Mrs. Pfeiffer, appears in the census of the population in that area, and at that time there were only two persons with the name of Pfeiffer close to Middletown, and one of them was a woman. Also, it appears that the Middletown School was a private school for girls in 1812, and turned public in 1813. Though there were no records kept prior to that date, this subject was genuine, and had no reason to commit fraud. In any case, it appears there is enough information given, up to now, that cannot be explained except by reincarnation.

Due to the fact that Doris G. did not appear and cannot be labeled as being a medium or a psychic, her information is quite relevant and fits statistically so many important documented details (over twenty of them), such as the geographical location, the residence, as well as where she was attending school, her age, the year that is so precisely defined, and corresponds to the 1810 census in Orange County, the name of the teacher in the Middletown School that appears correct, and the fact that there were only two people with that name in that area, and only one was a woman, Mrs. Pfeiffer, at a comparable age as

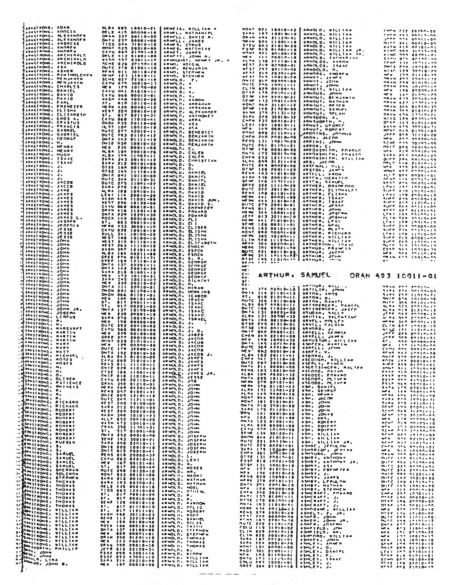

THE 1810 FEDERAL CENSUS

Samuel Arthur's name and the codes describing family members appear on the enlarged line above. Samuel Arthur's granddaughter, Lisa Arthur, fits the seventh digit in column four.

Fig. No 1

KEY TO THE 1810 FEDERAL CENSUS

The index to the 1810 census of New York is printed to four columns. The following paragraphs explain the meaning of each column with other necessary details for its use.

Column One

The first column lists in alphabetical order the name of the individuals found in the original census record. It should be understood that all of the names found therein are the heads of each household. The asterisk (*) following a name indicates that the spelling of the name is in question. When given names are abbreviated in the census and the abbreviation is clearly understood, the name is written out in the index.

Column Two

Column two contains a four-letter code which pertains to the counties. Each code uses the first four letters of the regular spelling of the county; thus RENS stands for Rensselaer County; ST stands for St. Lawrence County, MADI stands for Madison County; etc.

Column Three

The third column is the page number reference to the national archives microfilm publication.

Column Four

The next column is a set of numbers which refer to the number of individuals in the respective household. The first digit is the number of males under 10 years of age. The second digit is the number of males ages 10 but under 16. Third is the number of males 16 but under 26. Fourth is males 26 but under 45. Fifth is the males 45 and over. Sixth is the females under 10. Seventh is the females 10 but under 16. Also in the census but not in the index are numbers for females 16 but under 26, females 26 but under 45 and 45 and over. Also a number of other free persons in the household and another number of slaves in each household.

the age of a teacher. These acts are difficult to refute. The fact that Lisa could describe so vividly the surroundings where she lived, that could fit very easily the geographic location where the Hudson River is, adds to the completeness of the evidence. Also, she included in the family, the age and sex of all the members that appeared in the census of 1810, which are of great statistical significance. Names of dependents did not appear in the census of that time, only ages. (See figures la and lb!) In conclusion, the case of Lisa Arthur is one of those cases that come the closest to proving the possibility of reincarnation. Therefore, this case, like others in the literature that were demonstrated, proves once more that the explanation for such a phenomenon may be, according to our present knowledge, restricted only to the possibility of a past-life existence. The difference between this case and the other, stated in the literature, is in my own judgment, a difference that convinces me, because of my own undertaking of this experiment. Now, many other similar accounts in the subject of reincarnation that appeared in the literature throughout the years, have become more acceptable to me. Lisa Arthur is by no means the only case that could be practically identified as a case of reincarnation.

If this is true, as a physician and as a psychiatrist I feel compelled to make some philosophical reflections about the meaning of this extraordinary finding. It has changed a great deal the way I now look at illnesses, the way I look at current existence. It has changed the way I plan to understand my patients from now on, and people in general. It opens up horizons in terms of diagnosis and therapy, and if put in the context of helping humanity and helping suffering people, I think that efforts in verifying these truths could be worthwhile. Unfortunately, there are only a few fellow psychiatrists or physicians in other specialties, who are openly interested in this kind of research. Therefore, I encourage the medical community to investigate this matter, which may bring solutions to a great deal of the still unsolved problems that we physicians struggle with in our practice.

Another case that deserves attention because of its unusual findings, is of a volunteer who reported one of her previous lives under hypnotic regression as Marian C. She describes herself as being 15 years old. She said she was born on April 20, 1869, apparently in Talbott County, Georgia. What is interesting is that she claims her father, George Colbert, born March 30, 1847, was born in Campbell County, and he was a plantation operator. The census of the 1860's shows somebody by the name of George Colbert living in that county. It was striking to discover that on the map there is no Campbell County in the state of Georgia now. But at that time there was a Campbell County, it is now part of Fulton County, and the seat of the large city of Atlanta. I asked the volunteer whether she knew about that and she had no reason to tell a lie. She happens to be a co-worker of personal integrity. She never knew about the name Campbell County in Georgia, as she did not know of the name George Colbert. It is known, the Subconscious many times may give disguised answers. This report could indicate the possibility that this lady lived before, and was the daughter of George Colbert, who was born or lived in Campbell County. The name of George Colbert appears in the census of the state of Georgia of 1980 or 1870. It is the only name that appears at that time, and it is at that time in Talbott County.

Another type of research that proves to be quite fascinating concerns the recollections of an eight year old girl. Her name is Mary F. Without hypnosis, this girl could go into a past existence and give very detailed accounts. The session was tape recorded, like the others. She just covered her eyes, sat down, relaxed and printed on "the blackboard of her mind" that her name, Pavrah Lemgap, which she corrected later to Paula Liborio, age 23 or 24 years. The year was 1886. She gave her birthdate as February 18, 1862. Her birthplace was Tala, Mexico. She printed these names on the "blackboard of her mind," too. Her occupation was horseracing. I asked her what was the cause of her death, and she said she was killed in a horse race, when she slid and fell from her horse, fatally striking her head; she died on May 8, 1886. I continued and asked her how long she waited until she was born again In this lifetime. Without hesitation, or deliberation she replied, immediately: "86 years." She described the house in Tala, Mexico as being of a "funny" shape, very small. She would draw it later on. It was made of logs and ropes that held tile logs together. There were logs that were held together also in the roof, a string was on the top, keeping together the two slanted parts of the roof, and ropes were also on the sides... There was a window, some draperies there, very simple, and one door. (See Fig. No. 2!) The terrain and landscape consisted of grass and also dirt, there was a forest on the left side of the house, with very tall pine trees; the ground was covered also with thick hay.

Later on she drew for me a circle of houses. The houses of the neighbors, including hers, were arranged in a circle. She said in the middle of the circle of houses there were some rocks, little rocks, but nearby there was a big sea, or lake and she started spelling it for me "Chapara." (See Fig. No. 3!) Looking at the map we find there is no other name for a big sea or lake in Mexico that would fit that description and location except Chapala Lake.

She described a few flat hills. Her mother was portrayed as having long hair in a bun, and a long dress with an apron. She said mother mostly worked, she cleaned the house. She was a housewife. The father was not rich. Bald and tanned from the sun like Paula, he was dressed "not very pretty." He had a shirt, green jacket without sleeves. "He does not have a job, he did not learn a lot, he didn't have enough money for school, he helps people cutting wood, and clearing for them," etc. Paula had a sister and a brother, the sister was a teenager, about sixteen or seventeen years old, younger than Paula, the brother was older, about twenty-seven or twenty-eight years old and was not married. He was going to work in a large building. Paula mentioned that the family were close to one another, as they "don't have a lot of money," and they had to get along with each other. Paula got a job horseracing. She was not married as she was trying "to get money" to enter the horse race, "to win money" and help her family. Paula got along the best with her sister; she was always on Paula's side whenever "she got into trouble." She described the village where they lived as being a small one. Neighbors sold things to them, such as brooms, and Paula's family would borrow things to them. All of them were good friends; they were eating Mexican foods, as they were "Mexicans not Indians."

At this point I asked Paula to describe one of their dishes. She described a dish that looked "like a circle," and was sweet, maybe it was a dessert, "it is made out of fruit—bananas and

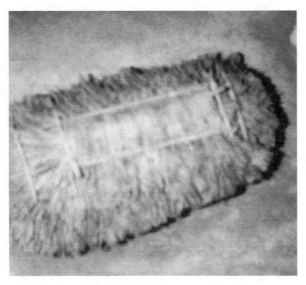

House made out of studs, tied up with strings as described by Paula Liborio. (Historical Museum — Guadalajara)

Fig. No. 2

Lake Chapala, surrounded by mountains, correctly described by Paula Liborio.

Fig. No. 3

pineapples covered with some white stuff, like cream." She claimed that they had always lived in the village. There was a game they often played. She described this game as being blue in color and was called Bocca. There are sticks and rocks, and the sticks are tied to the rocks; one holds onto the stick, and there is a rectangular board made out of wood; each player has a stick with a rock, glued at one end, and there is a rock in the middle of the board. The aim of the game is to see who can push the rock from the middle of the board with the stick, to the other players home base; whoever succeeds is the winner. Paula drew the game for me later on. In the Encyclopedia Britannica, "Boccie," is defined as an old Italian bowling game which is also played in Italian communities in the United States, Australia, and South America, and is very similar to "Bocca" as described by little Mary.

They used to make balls to play with as children; they made them out of wood and covered them with cloth, different colored cloth. Paula described to me a very sad event in her life: there was an old lady, a close friend, a woman in the neighborhood, that died of a heart attack. Also, she reported her grandparents' death. They made a grave for them nearby, and a headstone on the grave with white small rocks, spelling out their names, printed in white. Sticks were placed behind to hold the stone up.

When Paula died, she was buried like her grandparents, in a grave close to the houses. Paula described to me a Mexican coin of the time, and later she drew it; on one side it shows a village with several houses, and on the top is printed "Mexico." On the other side is a palm tree and again on the top is printed "Mexico." Paula said she prayed that she would have "a lot of money" by winning the race; she "tried praying a lot so G-d would help," but it did not. She named her Subconscious as "Paula" and said "Paula, entered the wrong body in Mexico." This life around, "Paula, entered the right body." This time she wants to live and have the abundance that she missed in the previous lifetime.

This is true, as she was born this time around to parents that can give her a life of abundance. She chose them this time because she claimed she was "fed up being poor. Paula described under my questioning, a special alcoholic drink called

"Pequira," and said it looks orange or yellow, and it is sweet, it contains lime juice and pineapple. Investigating the findings from this little girl, Mary, it appeared that a great deal of her information was authentic. First of all, what was very striking was that she gave the name of "Tala" as the place of her birth, which fits her description, as it is on mountainous terrain with pine trees and is close to Guadalajara, in Mexico, at an elevation of about 5,000 feet. She could also say, without deliberation, very fast for her age, without calculation, the right figures that added up and prove the validity of her claim. She said that she was born in 1862 and she died at age 24, which means she died in 1886. Then again, without hesitation, or time to calculate, she said rapidly that she waited 86 years to reincarnate. 1886 plus 86 makes 1972, when Mary was born this time around. When asked to say about any water, around the place where she lived, she spelled a name that was closest to Lake Chapala spelling, which is the largest lake in Mexico, and is quite close to the place where Paula lived, located as she described, "on the right" of her house — East and South. Her simple-minded account seemed so natural, that it is hard to believe it is made up. The names that she gave appear to be Spanish names, including her own name. The morals of that small society seem to be accurate and there is a Mexican food that looks like she described, it is a dessert circle-shaped, covered with cream and its name may correspond to "Flange." She could name the drink that was popular at the time, "Pequira." It appears that she slightly misspelled the name of "Tequila." The renunciation of Tequila, in Mexican, sounds like Mary gave it to me, which is "ira," instead of "Ila," the pronunciation of the L is like R, the same thing with Chapala which was spelled by her "Chapara." Besides, Mary could give me the composition of this drink; to my surprise, looking in the Encyclopedia Britannica, I found that these ingredients are used to make Tequila. The color of it is yellow, light orange, or straw colored. This case of Paula Liborio is very relevant. This provides an excellent example to support a theory of reincarnation. It is hard to assume that a child of eight years old, would bring such information so easily, and that this information would contain so many accurate details, as she never had any Mexican exposure in her present lifetime.

In retrospect, after a visit to Tala, Mexico, immediately prior to the completion of this book, I could check first hand in the Registrar of Baptism (Fig. 6 and 7) of Newborn children, in the only church in Tala, Mexico (listings since 1500's), three names of Paula, with "L," Liborio. (See Figures No. 4 and 5!) Only this one was baptized on January 30, 1862, the closest to February 18, 1862 that Mary related to me. Later on Mary confirmed that her real name was Paula Liborio and not only the name of her Subconscious. This appears in my experience a common occurrence when a name of a Subconscious is chosen because it is the name of the individual in a previous life. Mary could also identify a picture of Benito Juarez as "The President," of Mexico at the time. Moreover, she identified "Charro" as referring to female horse racing, that was popular at that time, and it can be verified in the book of Jose Alvarez del Villar, entitled Men and Horses of Mexico.

This is another amazing case that opens the real question of reincarnation as a plausible hypothesis. This girl does not have unusual psychic abilities, nor is she a medium by any means, and had no way to get this information in her current life. In the former life she was Catholic. In her present Jewish family she was never exposed to Mexican culture, therefore, her information seems to be accurate, simple, without flowers, and comes right from the source her memory bank, in her Subconscious. It was made accessible through this exercise of past life regression. This is an impressive case, though not unique of its type, because it is a well-known fact that usually children have a better memory for past-life facts than adults. Even if Doris G. or Mary F. had had psychic abilities, it is most improbable they would be able to describe with such accuracy, names, dates, places, events as they did, which again strengthens the reincarnational hypothesis, as the only explanation available now.

In Paula Liborio's case, her birthdate was February 18, 1862, (Sun sign-Aquarius), which corresponds to the Capricorn-North Moon's Node. In her current life as Mary F, she was born on July 22, 1972, (Sun sign-Leo), which also corresponds to the Capricorn North Moon's Node. In many past lives she was therefore experiencing in Cancer South Moon's Node. This implies in both lives this girl has been learning the same life

Fig. No. 4

Tala Church — Parroquia de Tala, Jalisco where Paula Liborio's Baptismal Certificate was found.

Fig. No. 5

An old picture of the Tala Church as it looked at the time of Paula Liborio and identified by Mary F.

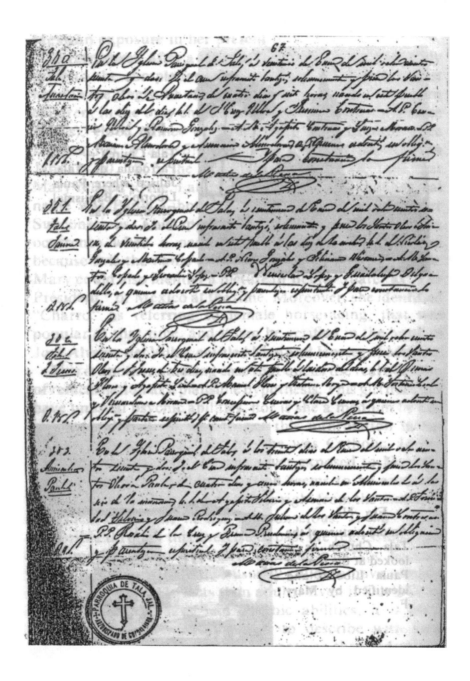

Fig. No. 6

APARTADO 1-331

Sr. Cura D. Rafael Hernández Morales.

Párroco de __Tala, Jalisco.__

CERTIFICA: que en el libro de Bautismos número __26.__

en la página _____ y bajo el número _____ se encuentra una acta del tenor siguiente:

En la parroquia de __Tala, Jalisco.__

a __30__ de __D Enero__

de __1862.__ el Pbro. __Sr. Cura Interino.__

bauti __zó__ solemnemente a __Paula.__

que nació el día __4 Días del mes de Enero 1862__ en __Ahuisculco, Jal.__

es hij __a Leg__ de __Agapito Liborio__

y de __Asención de los Santos__

Abuelos paternos __Trinidad Liborio__ __Juana Rodríguez.__

Abuelos maternos __Julián de los Santos y__ __Juana Contreras.__

Padrinos __Rosalío de la Cruz y__ __Bruna Prudencio.__

Notas marginales __No tiene.__

Y para los fines que convenga a __1__ interesad __o__ se expide el presente en __Tala, Jalisco.__ a los __21.__ días del mes de __Diciembre.__ de 19 __82.__

El Párroco

F. 105

Fig. No. 7

experience — the experience of Capricorn, which would logically make sense, as in the previous life she died prematurely. Therefore, she apparently did not get sufficient time to experience in the Capricorn North Moon's Node, long enough. That is why in this lifetime she is to repeat the same experience. This karmic astrological concordance in Mary F.'s case is another proof favoring the validity of her reincarnation.

Doris G.'s birthdate in her current lifetime is June 7, 1958, (Sun sign-Gemini), which corresponds to Libra North Moon's Node. As Lisa Arthur, born on December 11, 1799, (Sun sign-Sagittarius), she was experiencing in the Aries North Moon's Node, which is 180 degrees opposite to Libra North Moon's Node. It is fascinating in Paula's case, there was no shift in the life experience (Capricorn in both lives), but there was a 180-degree shift in the Sun sign from Aquarius to Leo; in Doris's case the shift from the previous life to the current life, 180 degrees both in terms of life experience (from Aries to Libra), and in terms of the Sun sign (from Sagittarius to Gemini). In Doris's case another characteristic is impressive, the life experience's sign and the sun sign, belong to the same element fire in the previous life, respectively, Aries and Sagittarius, and Air in the current life — respectively, Libra and Gemini.

Separate past life regressions of a mother and a daughter provided me with another support for the validity of reincarnation. Audrey G., the daughter, an attractive 23-year-old woman, confessed before she went into hypnotic regression that she had a tremendous fear of blood since she was a young child of three. She told me she faints at the sight of blood. Ironically, she serves in a clinic in one of Chicago's large hospitals. She told me that whenever she sees blood samples, she feels faint and repulsed. I asked her if she knew of any significant occurrence in her current lifetime prior to the age of three that could explain her morbid fear of blood. She could offer none.

During her regression, Audrey reported being a young three-year-old living on a farm in a small mountain village in the 1600's in Germany, near the Swiss border. One day she witnessed her mother being beaten by her drunken father. She then saw her father stab her mother with a knife. She could see the blood spilling over her mother's clothes and on to the ground. She ran to the barn nearby, where she hid trembling with fear. She told me that her present mother is the same mother who was killed by her father in that earlier life.

The daughter did not tell her mother anything that had transpired in her past life regression. The mother, Carmella, reported under hypnosis that there was some time in either 1572 or 1672 in a small mountain village in Germany that she bled to death because of a beating by her husband. She could see her frightened young daughter running to the barn.

The mother reported another lifetime as Mary Mueller, who was born on September 12, 1832, in a place called "Ogellaff, Switzerland." A map of Switzerland reveals that the only place close to that name is the town of Ogellingail. which is on the border between Germany and Switzerland. She said she married Paul Mueller at St. Joseph's Church on August 12, 1882. They had a daughter, Ann Mueller, born to them in 1856. Mary died on April 9, 1894, of "a cold." She claimed that the karmic connection again was Ann, who is her daughter Audrey in her present lifetime.

After all these findings, it is clear why Mary had such a strong fear of blood. The tremendous emotional pull towards her mother, due to fear that she might lose her again, can be explained as well. In turn, the mother began to understand the strong emotional attachment to her daughter.

A similar type of corroborative regression was found in the case of Linda A. and her daughter-in-law, Cindy A. Both women are intelligent individuals who realized the importance of not contaminating the research by communicating with one another about their own regressions.

These two successive and separate regressions revealed the following: 1. Both Linda and Cindy shared multiple previous lives together (8 - 14 lifetimes); 2. Gender roles were changed as well as types of relationship. 3. Both experienced emotional closeness throughout all the lifetimes shared together. 4. Both shared an affinity for certain countries (China, Egypt, Africa, India, England, and the U.S.). 5. In their common life spent in Africa Cindy was a female and Linda her husband. 6. In Egypt Cindy was the mother and Linda the daughter. Their relationships in other lifetimes revealed similar interchanging of roles — all of them close — which accounts for their strong emotional attachment to each other.

Another category of past-life regression has to do with the experience of strong emotions. It is quite difficult to prove objectively that strong emotions experienced under hypnotic regression are related to a past life. Yet those who experience such emotions are quite convinced of their validity and their origin in a past life — especially since it often explains current problems. It takes re-experiencing to strongly sense a past life.

Many times there is little doubt in the subject's mind that there was such a past life. The feelings experienced are too vivid to doubt the validity of their origin in the past.

One case that I found most intriguing was that of a young woman, Pamela, who had been treated by me earlier for attacks of extreme nervousness and anger. Pamela told me that she could not go into a past life. Although I worked hard to regress her into a past existence, it appeared that her subconscious was quite apprehensive. Through forceful insistence, however, I was able to regress her into a past life, while she trembled with emotion. After nearly an hour of silence, Pamela began talking. She introduced herself as Leslie Fairchild, age twelve, in the year 1863. The place in which she lives is New Haven, Connecticut. She then tells me the names of various members of her family. She tells me that she sees herself pressing her face against a window pane of her home, a frightened twelve-year-old. She is dressed for a special occasion with a green hat, and is expecting to go with her family to a country fair. The family is outside. Apparently they have forgotten to take her.

She says that a fire starts in the house, which is soon in flames. She feels the heat coming closer and closer. She is angry at her family that they have left her alone in this inferno. She is screaming, shouting, angry that nobody can hear her. The flames come closer and closer. The cracking noise of the burning wood becomes intolerable, the smoke suffocating. Ben, the handyman, comes to save her, but in vain. Everything collapses in flames. She is unable to tell me any more about the flames, though I urge her to do so. Though I insist, there is still silence. Finally the flames engulf her, despite her fight to escape the blaze. Though Pamela expressed a great deal of fear, I thought it important for her to experience to the fullest this trauma that had made her in the current lifetime so angry, impulsive and nervous, as therapeutic catharsis.

As the flames finally engulf her, her screaming and shouting begin to diminish, and she became calm. She said that as she died, she viewed her body from a position near the ceiling being burned by the flames. After she left the body she started to float and felt a relief.

When she came out of the trance, Pamela understood for the first time the reason for her anger, anger at her parents. She had felt completely frustrated. She had such beautiful plans, but absolutely everything was burned in the fire. Her family had forgotten her. After this learning reexperience, Pamela knew the source of her anger and resolved to conquer it in the future.

Another unusual category of regression that deals with emotions is related to people who died in the Second World War, in the Korean conflict, or in the Vietnam War. One such case is that of Ronald S.

Ronald was born in 1945 of a Christian family in Germany. He had been living in the United States after emigrating from Germany as a young child. Under hypnosis, Ronald disclosed that in a previous life, in 1938, his name was Henri Weisen, a Jew who lived in Wiesbaden, Germany. He said he was born in France on May 5, 1900. Ronald said he was a science teacher without a certificate and he wandered from place to place. He reported he lived during the time the Nazis came to power in Germany and that he and his wife tried to escape being sent to a concentration camp. At this point of the regression he suddenly became extremely emotional. He began to cry and shout. His body began to tremble.

"They are after us, they are after us."

"Who are they?" I asked.

"The soldiers."

"Who are the soldiers?"

"The German soldiers."

"Why are they chasing you?"

"What a question, what a question! I am a Jew! That is why!"

He ran, but the soldiers were getting nearer and nearer. Eventually he was shot, as was his wife.

What is interesting is that he chose to reincarnate this time as a German, rather than as a Jew. He did not wait for long. It

81

is not too unusual for those who die in war to reincarnate rapidly. In Ronald's case, the reincarnation occurred almost immediately after a seemingly unjust death; secondly, he decided to be born of the same nationality as his adversary in order, apparently, to avoid the fear of being killed again; thirdly, his emotional reaction was so vivid that Ronald could not deny its truth. Although science may find it difficult to accept the validity of such a case, the shattering emotion experienced by Ronald could not be denied, and certainly lent strong evidence for reincarnation.

A volunteer with an alcoholic problem by the name of Nancy volunteered for past life regression and revealed she was Analie Freeman, born March 12, 1817, in Batavia, Illinois, of American Indian parents. She was a member of St. Mark's Catholic Church in Cairo, a neighboring town. Analie said she was involved in the blackmail of a white man and a married woman, Josephine Hyman. Apparently the woman's husband was a high official at the state capital who had hired Analie as a housemaid.

Josephine Hyman was having an amorous affair with a certain Carl Weirrian. Analie told an Indian friend, John Blackwell, about it, and Blackwell blackmailed Carl Weirrian.

Analie was discovered in this plot by her tribe, who executed her by shooting an arrow through her chest. She felt betrayed by John, whose involvement in the blackmail she did not divulge.

In another life regression Nancy was named Maria. The year was 1622 in Pilgrim America. At sixteen she started indulging in drinking and prostitution. She died in a highly emotional state from alcoholism before she was 50. Under hypnosis she claimed that she had been an orphan raised by nuns. When sixteen, she met a young man who was "nice" to her. She "started sleeping" with him, but subsequently he disclosed his real self when he forced her to have sex with other men. In this way she became involved in prostitution, and because of the resulting anguish and emotional pain, she began to drink. When she re-experienced her death under hypnosis, she cried profusely, and it had a cathartic effect on her. Nancy was thus able to trace back her drinking problem in this lifetime.

Another case, that of Gary M., illustrates a condition that stems from a past life; in this case, nearsightedness. Under hypnotic regression Gary became Ted Arnold, who was 30 years old. He was born in 1809 in a town in Casper County, Wyoming. His mother died while giving birth to him.

Ted was an animal trapper by occupation. At the age of eight he moved with his father to "Medusa" in Kansas. (Medora, Kansas, appears to be the closest to the word "Medusa.") Ted did not remember the name of the school. At 16 he moved to "Summit Hole," in Burn County, Utah. It took him about a day on horseback to get there, where he lived in a cabin and raised horses. He married a Christy Smith at Calgary Church on October 10, 1836. Sometime later his wife was killed by an arrow. He had two children, a son and a daughter, who were born in 1838 and 1840 respectively. Ted died on November 10, 1865, from failing off a cliff, when he was thrown by a horse. He was buried by his son on their own land.

Another life of the subject was in 1687, as a musician, Derek Bucholtz. He played the organ at a Lutheran Church in Stuttgart, Germany.

In another life, in 1524, he served as a soldier in England. He said he was "crunched" with a sword across the temple. The sword moved so fast he could not see it. A relationship seems to exist between this experience as an English soldier and his current nearsightedness, in that there is a dissociation between vision and the thought connected to it. Therefore, the object or weapon is frozen very close to the eyes by the thought, which is faster than the vision. The actual sight is still far away.

This interesting hypothesis appears to be confirmed by another subject named Joan D., who was regressed to a time when she was a male by the name of Arthur. In the current lifetime Joan had been complaining of nearsightedness and pseudotumor cerebri, and had been treated for many years by neurologists and other doctors without major success. Pseudotumor cerebri is a condition in which the tissue of the brain is swollen through the accumulation of liquid. This happens especially in women who are on birth control pills or are pregnant, or patients on medications, and it may be life threatening. The sterol etiology is unknown.

During her regression to "Arthur Tucket," Joan reported that she was born November 1, 1918, in Osaka, Japan, where her father was serving on a United States military base, and returned to this country when the subject was four years of age.

Eventually Arthur became a horse trainer and worked at various race tracks. The father, Arthur Tucker, Sr. died when Arthur, Jr. was 18. His mother, Mary, died when he was seven.

After his father's death, when Arthur was 18, he worked with horses on the grounds of different racetracks, lastly in Baltimore, Maryland. On May 4, 1940, when he was 21, a fire broke out in the stables at the track and the horses trampled him to death. When recounting this, the subject became very emotional. He began to sob and his whole body trembled, as he experienced again the legs of the horses trampling him to death.

Joan reported another life as a twenty-year-old female in the year A.D. 16. She was condemned to die in a lion's cage, but she felt she was not guilty. It is not clear whether this was because of her belief in Christianity. In any case, she saw again a lion tearing her head with his paw. At this point, she began to cry and scream. This event was the one that triggered her current affliction of pseudotumor cerebri and nearsightedness. Obviously, related events reported in other lifetimes also contributed to the trauma to the head at close range.

It is remarkable to note that in both lifetimes there is a story of damage to the head. Apparently the subconscious fixated in those situations; since the above conditions were made conscious for the first time, reprogramming was possible by positive repetition programming. The patient's nearsightedness is a desperate attempt on the part of the subconscious to contain the deadly object or situation at close range, to stop it from becoming lethal. Obviously it was without success.

Another case deserving attention is that of Lillian. Regressed under hypnosis, she revealed herself to be Mary Duncan, 23, living in 1853. The place was a small village in Quincy County, Illinois. Her birth date was May 13, 1831. She died at 53, from freezing in cold weather. The feeling of coldness was re-experienced quite intensely in the trance state. This was a most dramatic session! She vividly experienced the sensation of coldness.

Some remarkable past life regressions of severely ill individuals deserve special attention. This case is typical.

Some patients with terminal cancer were referred to me for

hypnosis, in the hope of arresting their cancer — or possibly curing it. When such individuals were regressed into past lives, it was found that usually some very traumatic event had triggered the cancer in their current lifetime. The following is such a case:

Marla J., a forty-two-year-old married woman, mother of five children, suffered from a severe type of leukemia. Anticancerous drugs were of little or no help. When regressed hypnotically to a past life, it was revealed that she committed murder by spilling the blood of a man — by stabbing him to death. Thus she must pay the "debt" by having her own blood spilled. In the sessions that followed, we discussed the importance of paying her karmic debt by doing good deeds, instead of self-destruction. As a consequence, her cancer started improving. Two years later, it was still in remission.

Another case, this time of diabetes, high-blood pressure and menopausal symptoms, with severe depression, was treated with hypnosis and past life regression. In this case as well, the patient improved through an understanding of her subconscious, and by "making deals with it" to pay off previous sins through the doing of good deeds. Such therapeutic dialogue with the subconscious is extremely helpful. My research strongly indicates that most severe physical or emotional conditions of this lifetime appear connected to some traumatic event in previous lifetimes. Therefore, the importance of investigating past lives and discovering the origin of a particular condition seems to be of paramount importance. Once the emotions and the recollections are brought into focus, the patient becomes conscious of them; thus he or she is able to master them in a logical, constructive manner.

Many of the other regressions I have conducted add support to the strong possibility of reincarnation. As a physician and psychiatrist, I feel compelled to share this preliminary report with my colleagues in the field, as well as other professionals and laymen alike. It is hoped that by their comments and investigations, further progress can be made toward the truth — and the possible discovery of a cure for various illnesses.

Anything in medicine that works should be given full consideration. In my experience, regression therapy has been working. In case after case, patients got well only after they were regressed to a past life or lives and discovered the original precipitating factor. They were then taught to apply positive repetition programming, preferably through short self-hypnotic exercises, repeated often.

I cannot stress enough how important it is that such work be duplicated by as many qualified personnel as possible, not with cold scientific detachment, but in the spirit of enthusiasm and empathy.

The human element is of paramount importance in healing, in helping people overcome problems. If this element is missing, then the type of research I am discussing is doomed to fail. I have to repeat again that I have done my research with enthusiasm. It is very important to recognize this from the start. Critics might question such an apparently subjective approach. I can only respond by stating that enthusiasm is infectious. It finds its way into the subconscious of my volunteers, who contribute the material for research and healing.

II.   THE HEALING PROCESS

INTRODUCTION

The discoveries revealed in past-life regressions have served to inform us of a new dimension in understanding the states of illness and health. One can assume as well that there are other universal laws yet to be unveiled through the study of folklore, ancient secret wisdom, legends and stories that seem at first glance scientifically unacceptable. But this very treasure of knowledge holds the secret to uncovering these laws and utilizing them for the good of mankind.

First of all, time is a notion that man created to apply to his earthly experience. In reality, the universe is infinite and the infinite is beyond time. Hence, it would be preferable to regard so-called "past lives" as different and parallel existences of an individual, with the assumption that only one of them is being experienced now.

At this point, let us consider some practical medical reasons for accepting the possibility of reincarnation. First of all, how do we recall our past lives? To begin with, we must first accept the fact that besides a physical body, we have another body - a double body, as it were, around the physical one, and intermingled with each of its cells. This double body, or aura, can be photographed (at least partly) with a special type of photography that takes place in a high-intensity electrical field. Known as Kirlian photography, it was discovered by an electrician named Semyon D. Kirlian in Russia several decades ago, but has only recently stirred up a great deal of interest and research, especially behind the Iron Curtain. Through the Kirlian effect one usually obtains a brilliant colorful crown or corona around the object photographed. This appears to be the electromagnetic field or partial aura of the physical body. The Russians call it bioplasma.

According to a different hypothesis, this aura may extend from a foot to several yards away from the physical body. After the physical body dies, this ethereal body survives. Because it is an identical double of the physical body, it carries with it the memory bank from the old physical body to the new one in which it eventually incarnates. This explains how a person under hypnosis, by tuning into his subconscious memory bank, can reveal precise details of past lives. Usually these details can be validated through public records or other verifiable sources.

I must stress that throughout my research into past lives and psychic healing for the past seventeen years I have found time after time that illness originates in the aura, or consciousness, and then spreads to the physical body. Likewise, healing is first effected in the aura-consciousness, and then, after a certain time interval, spreads into the physical body. This seems to be a significant fact. Experiments with Kirlian photography, for example, show that when a leaf of a plant is infected with a plant virus, the illness occurs first as patchy black shadows in the aura. Only after a certain interval of time, perhaps hours, is the physical leaf affected. During the process of healing, the sequence is reversed; first the aura becomes clear, then the physical leaf. The phantom limb phenomenon is hereby illustrated as the aura continues to exist after the ablation of a portion of the leaf.[40] (See Fig. No. 8)

Modern medicine, as we know it, is about four hundred years old. It is based mainly on Newtonian, reductionistic concepts, which regard "scientific" only what can be perceived and demonstrated through the organs of sense. It is regrettable that medicine still builds many of its notions on this reductionistic view, and still treats the body-machine at the expense of neglecting consciousness.

Fortunately, Einstein gave us the Theory of Relativity, and established the formula $E=MC^2$. In other words, energy and matter are interchangeable. Energy equals matter multiplied by the square of the speed of light. Therefore, whatever is now solid, presenting a thicker level of energy vibration, may become thinner later on as well as the reverse. Uranium is a solid metal and it is common knowledge how, under certain circumstances of fission, it disintegrates into a thinner form of energy with awesome power. Though the organs of sense cannot detect directly this form of energy, the end result is undeniable. By the same token, the aura-consciousness is as important, not more important, than the physical body and requires an understanding for the betterment of man.

It is not uncommon that when a person has to make an

important decision a great deal of internal feuding takes place. One part of the consciousness may say, "I want to do it now!" while the other part might reply, "No, it is too early. Let us weigh the facts first." Then the other part screams.

Unfortunately, that impulsive, childish, animal part of consciousness, which is the subconscious, is allowed to have its way. Fortunately, chaos is prevented. For behind all beauty is creation, a force of inexhaustible and infinite power, which dwells in all forms. This is the Higher Self or the Superconscious.

Fig. No. 8

CHAPTER SEVEN
The Kahunas and Consciousness

Any study of our behavior will most certainly require a parallel study of consciousness; the two are inextricably bound together. As a psychiatrist specializing in regressive hypnosis, I have long been concerned with human consciousness. This interest has led me to initiate a broad range of studies, most of which have been fruitful; a few sadly disappointing.

One such fruitful study has been that of the Kahuna priests of the Hawaiian Islands. The word *kahuna* is formed from two Hawaiian words: *ha*, keeper, and *huna*, secret. Obviously, the implication here is that the Kahunas are guardians of some type of esoteric knowledge. The implication is well founded.

"Knowledge is a function of being," wrote Aldous Huxley, but not every being is suited for every kind of knowledge. Some information is best left in the hands of those sufficiently developed to understand and propagate it, and this premonition the Kahuna priests have obeyed.

Basically, the Kahuna philosophy rests upon the acceptance of three levels of consciousness or "selves": Higher Self, Middle Self, and Lower Self. Lower Self might be said to be equivalent to the subconscious mind. The Kahunas call it *Uhinipili*, which we shall later see contains a significant root meaning.

The Lower Self is regarded by the Kahunas as completely autonomous, and programmed to control the various processes of the physical body. In a sense, it serves the other, higher spiritual selves. The Lower Self is composed of a thinner, finer energy vibration than the physical body, or *aka*, which the Kahunas describe as a mold of cells, tissues, and organs. It is also the seat of the emotions and produces a vital force, or *mana*, which is used by the other two selves. In addition, it is the function of the Lower Self to receive impressions through the organs of sense and record these impressions upon what the Kahunas call the "shadowy body" - composed of a finer form of energy than the physical body.

Words, images, sounds and thoughts occur in trains of time units; composed of multiple single impressions clustered together. The Kahunas view these as symbolic clusters, of microscopic size, impregnated in a part of the Lower Self which is best described as the brain's "double." At death the subconscious, in its aka body, departs the body and brain, taking with it all memory of the past life.

According to the Kahunas, the subconscious can be influenced and controlled by hypnosis, since thought forms can be implanted in its aka body through effective suggestion. The subconscious has definite control over the vital force (*mana*) and of any form of use of its aka substance. In addition, the subconscious is able to hold thoughts and ideas in its aka substance as memory in the form of word-picture clusters (which for some reason, the conscious mind does not get a chance to rationalize). It reacts to such a fixation-complex so powerfully that the conscious mind is unable to control it. As a result, problems arise.

The latent capabilities of the subconscious mind are of exceeding interest to the Kahuna priests, which will become apparent in the passages to follow. These abilities of the Lower Self are:

1.   The capability to feel radiation from objects when the nature of this radiation cannot be registered by the five senses; in other words, extrasensory perception.

2.   The ability of the subconscious to attach itself to a person or object by an invisible subtle thread created from its aka substance. The root word, *Pili* (Lower Self), also means "sticky." This connective thread originates first through either visual or bodily contact, and then remains more or less permanently fastened to the aka ectoplasm at the region of the solar plexus.

Later on the Lower Self can project a finger-shaped aka substance. By following this "thread" it is possible for the Lower Self to locate and contact again the person or thing at the other end of the thread. With each contact, the thread becomes stronger, its permanence enhanced, and it is easier to follow.

3.   Another latent capability involves use of the aka threads. First, the so-called aka finger projection, along the formed thread, can take with it part of the aka double of the sensory organs. This is why after death life continues in the shadowy body made of aka substance. All sensory organs are duplicated

in its ectoplasm, functioning precisely as they do in the physical body. During astral projection, all of the aka body is projected a prescribed distance; there it uses the organs of sense as though the physical body were present. Even though the aka finger that is projected is a small part of the whole aka body, it can still make use of all the senses in obtaining impressions of the person, object, or place it has contacted. These impressions can be referred back along the thread and shown to the conscious mind.

Second, there is a reversing of the train of impressions along the binding aka finger or aka cord. In other words, impressions can be transmitted in reverse as well. These impressions are changed from the actual sensory reality of the objects to thought-forms or thought-pictures of them. These are microscopic impressions imprinted on tiny bits of aka substance. A few of them can be joined to form a cluster which can convey the thought content. Transmitting these thought-picture clusters is known as telepathy.

According to the Kahunas, it is imperative to train the subconscious to use the above-described natural qualities, for all forms of prayer are telepathic. They also emphasize this training in order for prayer to be effective. In the Bible, G-d is described as Spirit. The Kahunas agree, adding that G-d within Man, or the Higher Self, is spirit. They state that only the subconscious and the conscious mind live in the high density of physical bodies. The Higher Self is not endowed with organs of sense; therefore, no matter how loudly one cries, the Higher Self will not hear.

The Kahunas send their prayers in thought-form clusters through the telepathic aka cord between the Lower Self and Higher Self, apparently bypassing the Middle Self. This appears to not be totally accurate. The Soul of Man - the Middle Self or conscious being - is certainly closer to G-d in the attributes of intelligence and will power than is the animal part of man, the Lower Self. As a matter of fact, the Middle Self, created in the image of G-d, forms an indissoluble unit with G-d through the connective aka cord. Therefore, communication between the conscious mind and the superconscious appears quite logical. If anything, the conscious-superconscious unit communicates better with the low mentality of the subconscious through thought-form clusters. Moreover, this puts the intelligence and will power of the conscious mind in full command of its earthly experience, whether in the physical body or in its absence.

Another modification I found throughout my investigation into reincarnation and psychic healing is the existence of the vital force, or mana, referred to by the Kahunas. When this energy derives from the Higher Self, it is known as *mana mana*. In order to obtain mana mana, one has to transmit energy from the Lower Self to the Higher Self. It seems illogical that the Higher Self needs the reduced energy of the Lower Self to help in prayer. If anything, the Lower Self needs the energy to perform as instructed by the Middle Self. The Higher Self derives its energy from the infinite, inexhaustible cosmic source within itself, which it will use for spiritual, creative or healing purposes on the physical plane if asked to do so by the Middle Self.[32]

CHAPTER EIGHT
The Healing Process

Healing occurs when, through one or more processes, a harmonious relationship is effected between the conscious and subconscious minds. With this definition in mind, let us examine five distinct types or categories of healing of which we know to be generally acceptable to healers. These are: 1. Pranic or magnetic healing; 2. Psychic or mental healing; 3. Spiritual healing; 4. Mystical healing; and 5. Divine healing. In practice, these various types of healing tend to overlap. Among these, spiritual healing comes closest to what has commonly become known as faith healing. Each category of healing has its distinct characteristics, methods, and practitioners.

Pranic or magnetic healing is a form of healing in which the healer sends a supply of *prana* or psychic energy to the affected parts of the patient, thus stimulating the cells and tissues to normal activity. In addition, waste matter is ejected from the body.

According to Indian philosophy, prana is the universal force or vital energy which stimulates all body activities. Pranic or magnetic healing is usually accomplished by either the passing over or laying of hands on the affected parts of the patient. This is an ancient practice. In Egypt, early rock carvings depict healers treating patients by placing their hands on the body.

What is the mechanism by which magnetic healing works? The right and left hands of the healer act like opposite poles, similar to those in an electric battery, to discharge prana. The healing takes place as it induces changes in the physical body by altering the flow of vital energy in the etheric body. Mary Howell, M.D., associate dean at Harvard Medical School, did extensive research into this form of healing. She observed that therapeutic touch can become a most powerful healing method.

Dolores Krieger, a professor of nursing at New York University, has also emphasized how the laying on of hands elicits deep relaxation in the patient, and is usually successful in relieving pain. Passing the hands over the patient, the healer may detect asymmetrical differences between the left and right

97

sides of the body. These differences are commonly described as "buzzing," "hot," cold," "touch," "dead," and so forth.[33]

Usually, irregularities over painful areas include a buzzing or jangling sensation; a deadness or coolness over the midback near the adrenal gland (which is in charge of stress-coping mechanisms) when the patient is experiencing stress or fatigue; irregular warmth in areas of inflammation or infection. Also, there may be a sensation of blockage of the energy flow in one or both of the extremities.

After assessing the problem, there comes "unruffling." The healer focuses energy into the patient to smooth out or "unruffle" those irregularities found during the examination. Next, is energy modulation.

This entails channeling blue energy through visualization in order to cool inflammation and for pain relief. Yellow energy is used to stimulate regenerative growth; green is used to replace tissue; red to initiate energy in the healee; and white is used as a disinfectant, as well as a powerful healing energy. In addition, white is the combination of all colors in the spectrum and acts as the interaction between the sun light and earth's magnetic vibration.

When the patient's field is sensed to be smooth, the healer concludes the treatment.

Dolores Krieger began promoting therapeutic touch some years ago in the graduate nursing program at New York University. Her students were considered somewhat "crazy." Today therapeutic touch practitioners are not any longer considered crazy, for thirty-three university hospitals now offer programs in magnetic healing (called "The Touch") and it is applied in many university medical centers.

Western science is still not terribly accepting, however. The Cartesian approach, which emphasizes an empirical view of life and separation of healer and healee, could prevent an understanding of the ways healing energy works. Healers know that the universal healing power, not their own, does the healing.

Philippine healer Jaime T. Licauco cites an interesting case of magnetic healing in which the patient, a woman, had developed a cyst on her right breast. Without touching the affected area, the healer made magnetic passes of his hands over the whole body. After three sessions, the cyst gradually disappeared. Before this happened, two medical doctors had examined the woman's breast. Although they both declared the cyst to be most probably benign, they advised surgical removal. "If we had not been aware of an alternative form of healing, we would have agreed," Licauco said.

In my own practice I have discovered that when using magnetic passes, I do indeed practice a certain type of therapeutic hypnosis in which verbal suggestions arc not always necessary. Healing energy is transmitted telepathically from the healer's conscious mind (or through his subconscious) to the healee's subconscious. It can be transmitted by actually touching the physical body of the patient, which is one to three inches away, or from great distances. This will be described later.

Anton Mesmer, the French physician and the founder of modern hypnosis, used the magnetic approach over a hundred years ago. He called the vital force he used in healing, "animal magnetism," and postulated that if the physician is more highly charged with the energy than the patient, the energy will flow from his body to that of the patient. Often he caused such a great charge of vital force, to enter the healee that shaking, fluttering hysterical fits or even unconsciousness resulted. This unconsciousness was confused with sleep, but it was something very different. In any case, it gave rise to the belief that mesmerism and sleep were somehow related.

Working on this problem of mesmeric sleep, Dr. James Braid in England made what he considered a remarkable discovery. He claimed that "suggestion" may produce the same artificial sleep. Moreover, by having a subject stare in a certain way at a bright object held above eye level, he found he could induce this form of sleep without the use of either suggestion or "magnetic force." Because of his lack of knowledge about the real mechanism of mesmerism, Braid did not realize that some vital force is always contained in suggestion; nor did he realize that a suggestion can be given silently, just by expecting the patient to fall asleep when asked to stare at a bright object which would tire the eyes. Usually tiring of the eyes leads to natural sleep. As a consequence of the suggestion, or the effect of a charge of vital force directed by the will, the induced sleep is artificial.

In my own practice of hypnosis over the past twenty-eight years, I have made sure that the radiations of energy I absorb from the higher force would eventually flow through me by a direct conscious channeling to the patient, making my verbal suggestions that much more powerful. Indeed, the results I obtained in 80 to 90 percent of the cases confirmed this fact. Invariably, magnetic healing has been a rewarding experience for me, especially in the relief of pain. Although the pain at times recurs, repetition of treatment helps greatly, and sometimes finding the subconscious conflict behind the pain and involving the patient in the process of self-help eventually results in a cure of the underlying condition.

It appears to me this is a universal law and, when abided by, brings about healing. The importance of knowing these laws is utilizing them positively, rather than becoming subject to their potential negative effects, directly or through omission. The above understanding has enabled me to channel healing from the higher force for many conditions previously thought incurable; humbly, by knowing how to utilize Nature's gifts according to well-established universal laws.

CHAPTER NINE
Mental Healing

Let us now discuss another type of healing - psychic or mental healing. This is the process by which the mind of the healer restores to normal condition the diseased organs by placing them under the control of the patient's mind. Successful psychic and absent treatments depend upon some level of telepathic harmony between the practitioner and patient. This type of energy vibration transmission may have not only communicative, but curative powers, as well.

During the process of psychic healing, the healer mentally contacts the subconscious of the patient, visualizing an image of the patient. He impresses upon it a normal condition or mental attitude, usually through picture-thoughts. At the time of treatment the healer raises his vibrations until they reach the proper level and then transmits them to the subconscious of the patient, resulting in the reproduction of these vibrations in the subconscious. The consequence is that the subconscious of the patient gradually re-establishes normality. Jonathan Cohen, using Kirlian photography, took pictures of thoughts. (See Fig. No. 9)[38]

Most healers elevate their energy vibrations through meditation; others might use a specific chant. If psychic healing is done with the patient not physically present, it is called absent healing. Its effectiveness can be the same as with the patient present. If there is genuine love and care for the patient, the healer can raise his vibrations and form a positive and clear mental image of the healee. This may be the determining factor in the success or failure of the treatment.

Mrs. O., a 47-year-old married woman suffering from severe menopausal symptoms, called me one night in a state of extreme panic. She thought her blood pressure excessive and she had chest pain radiating to the left arm. I told her on the phone to relax and close her eyes. Then I asked her to wait as I was going to send her absent healing.

I began to form a clear and positive image of her on the screen of my mind. I focused on her hypophysis gland, seeing it with

101

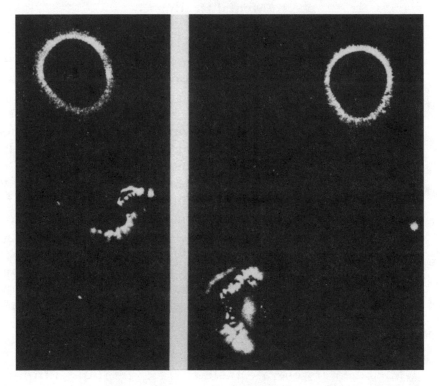

Electrophotograph of telepathic "M"
Electrophotograph of telepathic "7"

Fig. No. 9

my mental eyes. Afterwards, I passed my imaginary hands up and down over this gland as I felt it to be unbalanced; at the same time, I bathed it in clear blue energy in order to calm it down. I proceeded the same way with her adrenal glands, which I could see in my mind, being situated on the upper poles of the kidneys. Then I bathed all of her body in blue energy, including her heart and circulatory system. At the same time, I visualized her blood pressure down to normal: 120/70 and her pulse at 70 per minute. Following this, I concentrated powerful white energy on the hypophysis, adrenal glands, heart and blood vessels; finally, I bathed her in bright white light for one or two minutes.

The healing took about three to four minutes, after which I asked Mrs. 0. how she felt. She told me that her pain disappeared, as did the pain in her arm. She felt relaxed and totally well. Bewildered she asked me: "What did you do? Did you perform magic?"

The next day she came to my office, and I found her good condition to be unchanged. I taught her how to do the healing herself, in the same manner as my treatment, and to repeat it every four hours during the day for as long as needed.

Spiritual healing is a form of healing in which the healer becomes merely an instrument. The healing power of the universe usually passes through the aid of discarnate spirits, or guides. One of these spirits is the spirit of G-d, or the Higher Self, within the individual. In both magnetic and psychic healing, the healer feels the power to be stored within himself. In spiritual healing, however, the power is to be conceived as outside the healer. Three well-known spiritual healers were the late Kathryn Kuhlman of the United States, Jose Arigo of Brazil, and Harry Edwards of England.

CHAPTER TEN
Psychic Surgery: Fact or Fiction?

In 1973 a group of distinguished scientists, physicians, engineers and psychic researchers visited the Philippines as members of a comprehensive research team. Their purpose was to impartially observe and later report on a number of Filipino faith healers or psychic surgeons. They conducted their research with commendable thoroughness and objectivity. At the close of their trip, they published the following statement, which I quote in part: "During our stay in the Philippines, we the undersigned, alone and in small groups, observed the activities Of several healers. Each of us, reporting only as an individual and not on behalf of any organization with which we may be connected, hereby confirms that psychokinetic phenomena which we observed during the healing activity:

1. Did not involve fraud.
2. Utilized no anesthesia.
3. Did not use scalpel, razor blades, or other instruments to open the body.
4. Required usually from one to ten minutes to perform.
5. Permitted in most cases the healer and patient to remain in street clothes, with no special precautions to maintain sterile conditions.
6. Appeared to cause little, if any, discomfort to the patient.
7. Left the patient without operative shock.

In their closing statements, the group reported that they did not feel it was "within the scope of this initial study to assess the effectiveness of the spiritual healing." However, they did admit to having witnessed hearings, though they were unable to offer an explanation for them. Interestingly enough, two of the panel's members had undergone spiritual hearings themselves in prior visits to the Philippines.

Unfortunately, the statement of the group was bitterly attacked by the European medical community, forcing many members of the group to remain silent for fear of professional ostracism.

Nearly nine years later, in January 1981, I decided to visit the Philippines myself and personally investigate - as a scientist - this controversial healing art. Through a combination of persistence and the kindness of several Filipino healers, I was able to witness many of the facts reported by other responsible observers. My acceptance of psychic surgery should not be construed as an endorsement, though I would not hesitate to recommend it in certain types of cases.

Because psychic surgery defies most accepted scientific laws, or appears to, traditional medicine tends to regard it as some type of trickery or sleight-of-hand, despite overwhelming evidence to the contrary. Psychic surgery is a fact. But it belongs to an order of reality that is not yet fully understood by modern science. This does not mean that such a reality is nonexistent; on the contrary, it simply cannot be assessed by the usual empirical methods.

Psychic surgery is not confined to the Philippines. Jose "Ze" Arigo, of Brazil, in the late 1960's, used a dull knife to perform psychic surgery. Certain rudimentary forms of psychic surgery are also performed in some parts of Indonesia, Africa, and the Amazon Valley. But only in the Philippines is it practiced to any large extent. Also, Filipino faith healers are the only ones to use their bare hands when operating on a patient. Although there are a large number of faith healers in the Philippines, no more than thirty or thirty-five among them are true psychic surgeons.

In the Philippines itself there exists an important religious organization which probably accounts for that country's high concentration of healers. It is the *Union Espiritista Christianade Filipinas*, founded at the beginning of this century as an organization dedicated to training healers. It numbers about 10,000 members, drawn mostly from Northern and Central Luzon. They are primarily taught the methods of communicating with the spirit world.

This most unusual "union" is responsible for developing several types of mediums. There are those who are able to predict the future; others who can talk to the spirits; and still others who develop healing powers. A small, highly select group is given the power to perform a material operation or psychic surgery. According to one authority, Jaime T. Licauco, "it takes many years of study and practice before one becomes a 'medium operator,' if at all."[34] (Many of the psychic surgeons, however, have left the Union and founded their own spiritist churches.) The Union discourages its members from charging money for their services, but it accepts donations in the name of the group for the welfare of the individual healer. Many of the healers have lately adopted a policy of commercialism with the apparent rationalization that a fee for service is an honest and acceptable practice. As everywhere, there will be a few who would practice dishonesty, misrepresenting their qualifications in order to gain profit.

What exactly is psychic surgery? Investigators have long been attempting to determine the validity of this type of healing. A number of scientific investigations have been conducted by scientists from throughout the world: Sigrum Seutemann and Dr. Alfred Stetler of Germany; Dr. Hiroshi Motoyama of Japan; Dr. Lyall Watson of South Africa; Dr. Hans Naegeli-Osjord of Switzerland; and Dr. Jesus Lava of the Philippines Society of Psychic Research, to name just a few.

As we mentioned earlier, psychic surgeons have been observed, investigated, and studied in regard to their methods. Laboratory tests of the tissues obtained through the investigations have also been conducted. In short, many scientists have become convinced of the genuineness of this phenomenon and the sincerity of the healers.

In the early and mid-1970's there were American newspaper reports that claimed Filipino psychic surgeons were substituting chicken and pig livers for real human organs. "These reports," states Licauco, "were given wide publicity both here and abroad. This in part accounts for the negative image of our healers. The story has persisted despite growing solid evidence to the contrary."

To support the healers' claim, South African biologist and psychic researcher, Dr. Lyall Watson, related an experiment in order to finally remove much of the doubt about the authenticity of psychic surgery. In that experiment both healer and patient were requested to be completely naked while the operation was being performed. The tissue obtained was then proved to be real human tissue from that particular patient, and the blood of a group appropriate to that patient.[35] In any case, thousands of patients, many of them declared incurable in their country of origin, continue to flock to the Philippines. The most credible sources claim 80 percent success in a population of patients that were generally considered to be treatment failures in their own countries.

How does psychic surgery work? Careful study by a Japanese scientist has revealed some fascinating facts. According to the observations of Dr. Hiroshi Motoyama, the healer's psychic energy, accumulated through concentration in the astral body, is able to transcend, as it were, the physical dimension. When the psychic surgeon emits the energy of the astral body through his fingers or palms, he temporarily eliminates the physical energy of the patient's body.

In modern physics, matter is considered to be a condensed form of energy. If the body's physical energy can be extricated by the power of the astral body of the healer, a portion of the physical body — a condensed mass of physical energy — may also be extricated. Therefore, the psychic surgeon is able to dissolve skin or tissues covering diseased areas by emitting spiritual energy from his hands. As a consequence, this skin or tissue ceases to exist, though temporarily. This explains how a surgeon's hands can freely enter the patient's physical body at any point. This paranormal ability is rare, however, and Tony Agpaoa (perhaps the most famous psychic surgeon) was one of these few able to perform such feats.

The psychic surgeon materializes outside the body blood and tissue from the patient, which can be obtained *through or without insertion of hands in the physical body*. In other words, the sick tissue which was transformed into a thinner form of energy vibration, is brought back to the initial form of energy vibration — the physical tissue and blood, but this time outside the physical body.[36] (See Figures No. 10-19. Photos (Fig. 10 and 11) courtesy of *Healing in the Philippines* by J. T. Licauco.)

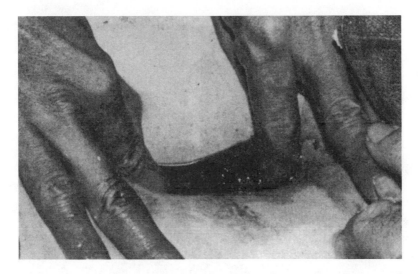

Enlarged shot of an "opening." Clearly fingers are going inside. (Photo by Henri Clement)

Fig. No. 10

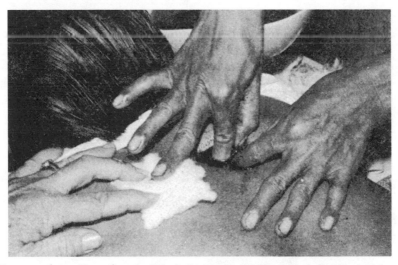

Close-up shot of bare-handed back "operation." Fingers definitely inside and cannot be bent backwards. (Photo by Henri Clement)

Fig. No. 11

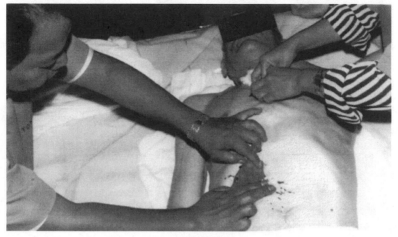

Psychic surgery to cure liver condition.

Fig. No. 12

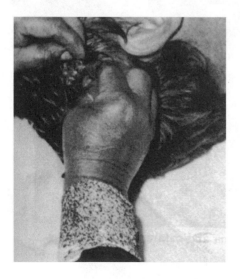

Operation on a
brain tumor.

Fig. No. 13

Fig. No. 14

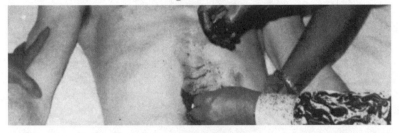

Operation on the pancreas on a patient with Diabetes Mellitus.

Fig. No. 15

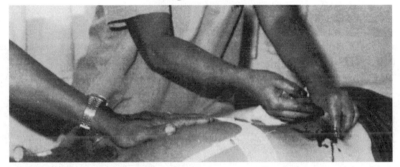

Removing a kidney stone.

Fig. No. 16

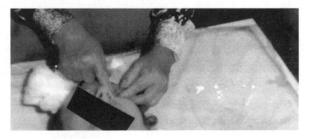

Operation on glaucoma and cataract of the left eye.

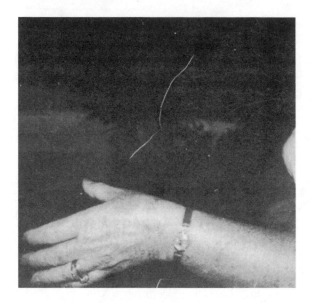

Fig. No. 17

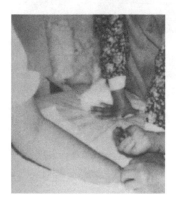

Fig. No. 18

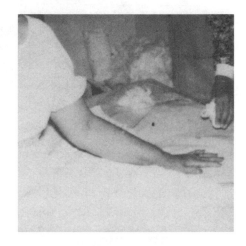

Fig. No. 19

Operation on basal cell carcinoma — starting with the upper picture: before, during and after the surgery.

CHAPTER ELEVEN
Tony Agpaoa – The Saintly Surgeon

In her book *Two Weeks With The Psychic Surgeons*, Marti Sladek describes the incredible story of her journey to see the Filipino healers who operate with their hands without instruments, anesthesia, scars, hypnosis, or pain. In an appealing, down-to-earth way, she relates many of the psychic surgeries she and her husband witnessed during their two-week trip to the Philippines.

In one fascinating account, she described how Tony Agpaoa operated on her father-in-law's heart:

> The operation on Dad's heart was undoubtedly the most dramatic of any we witnessed on the trip, it was also one of the longest lasting, well over ten minutes. Dad was on his back on the bed, Tony knelt beside him and went into a trance, praying half-aloud in English and Tagalog, asking for the power to be channeled through him to do G-d's healing work. His hands hovered over Dad's chest momentarily, then plunged in. Suddenly, he jabbed his right hand, palm up, under the rib cage. When he pulled it out, he was holding Dad's heart in his hand, lifted slightly out of the chest cavity. He had used no instruments. Dad was wide awake; I asked him if he felt anything, and he said "no" - yet we could see his heart beating in Tony's hand. Tony called for a towel, which Robbie laid over Tony's hands. Now we couldn't see what he was doing. I shut the cameras off while he worked in trance under the towel for perhaps eight minutes, then Robbie whisked the towel off at a nod from Tony. I clicked it back on. Tony was pulling goop out of the blood vessels around the heart. He dropped the stringy, whitish stuff into a pan of water, saying it was cholesterol and fat deposits. Robbie emptied the dish into the toilet. Don had walked in just in time to see his father's heart in Tony's hand, well out of the chest, his mouth dropped open. Something terrible was happening - as soon as Don

113

entered the room, the vibration changed; there was an instant enmity between him and Tony, partially, we're sure, because Tony was miffed at Don for not being there right from the start, and partially something much deeper, perhaps Karmic in nature. . . Tony quickly finished with Dad, placing the heart gently back down in its nest, removing his hands and massaging briefly where the opening had been. Robbie followed with a short treatment with a battery-powered vibrator which Tony claimed would stimulate the circulation.[37]

Rosita Rodriguez is a famous spiritual healer, psychic surgeon, and close associate of Tony Agpaoa. She presently lives in Oak Park, Illinois. In a fairly recent interview with author David St. Claire, she was asked about the "real" story behind Tony not being allowed into the United States. Rumor stated he was accused of fraud or of taking money for a healing he never performed.

Rosita said it all began:

> ...when a construction worker by the name of Joe Ruffner fell off a scaffold and fractured his spine in several places. This accident happened in Wyandotte, Michigan, in 1956. He was taken to a veteran's hospital and they operated on him. Though doctors treated him for twelve years, they were unable to get him to walk or to move his arms; he was completely paralyzed. He had been on narcotics for so long that they had lost their effect, and his pain had become nearly unbearable. The doctors told him the only thing they could do was to sever his spinal cord.
>
> This time he balked, he drew the line at having this drastic surgery. Then he heard about Tony in the Philippines and wrote to him. He told Tony what was wrong, but added he didn't have any money to pay him. Tony wrote back and said he only lacked faith and that with faith he would somewhere find the cash for the airplane ticket. Tony said he wouldn't charge him for the operation. So Joe told his parish priest about Tony's offer and much to his amazement the priest talked the congregation into taking up a collection and sending Joe

over to the Philippines. Faith had paid for the trip.

The first time Tony worked on him he told him to get up off the table and stand on his own two feet. Joe said it was impossible, that he hadn't been able to stand for twelve years. Tony insisted and slowly he sat up, swung his legs off the table and stood up. Then Tony said,'Okay, Walk!'Joe took a few steps and with just a little bit of help was able to walk across the room and back. He had several other operations after that, and when his plane arrived in the United States, he walked down the steps and ran to embrace his sobbing wife.

Joe went back to the veteran's hospital and told them he was cured. He asked to be taken off the disability paychecks and given a medical release so he could get a job and earn his own money. The doctors refused; they said he wasn't cured, that there was no way he could be cured even though they saw him walking and using his arms. So they took x-rays and showed him that *nothing* had changed. His spinal column was still broken, but Joe insisted that he was cured. He ran up and down a staircase for them, he threw and caught a ball for them. He tried to convince them that no matter what the bones showed, the nerves were perfect again and he was cured.

While he was battling for a medical release, word traveled fast in his church group that he had gone to Tony and been cured. Others in the area also wanted to be cured of various ailments, and they asked Joe to organize a trip to the Philippines for them. He made the necessary arrangements with Tony and obtained a special charter flight with a Canadian airline. The flight left Canada with people in wheelchairs, on crutches, and with great hopes. But the American Medical Association heard about this load of sick Americans they could not cure, heading over to a foreign faith healer, and they were furious. They notified the Philippines Medical Association and demanded action be taken. The patients who had come so far didn't care what the AMA or the PMA thought. They wanted to be cured, and almost all of them were!

When they returned to the United States the AMA was right after them. What did Tony do? What cures did he effect? How much money did he swindle out of them? And so on and so forth. Most of the ten people on that flight told the AMA "to bug off," but there were a few who had not been healed or else who had had their illness return after they arrived back in the States, the AMA got these few to sign statements against Tony. What they really were jubilant about was that they thought they had a case against him for transporting U.S. funds across the border because the money for the charter flight had been sent from Michigan to Canada. If Joe had been able to get an American flight they wouldn't have had a leg to stand on. It must be remembered that it wasn't Tony's idea to set up the flight or to choose a Canadian airline over an American one. He was in the Philippines, and all the arrangements were made here in the States.

Well, the next time that Tony arrived in San Francisco he was arrested. He was accused of transporting funds across the border. We immediately got him a lawyer, and put up bail. The lawyer proved that the money was sent by check from one bank to another and that everything was perfectly legal. While this was being decided some of his more loyal followers decided to make a test case out of it, to make the AMA accept Tony here in the United States once and for all. There was publicity in the papers and the poor man was dragged around and discussed both pro and con. With all this publicity, and all this uproar, Tony felt lost and very much a foreigner in a strange land. So he did a silly thing, he skipped the country, he jumped bail!

There had been no evidence against him on any of the counts and the case would have been thrown out, if it had come to court. Tony didn't want to wait for the slow moving judicial system to operate. He went back to his own country and because he jumped bail, he is technically a fugitive to be arrested whenever he returns.[38]

I had the good fortune to meet Tony Agpaoa and observe his so-called "miraculous" feats of psychic surgery, as well as photograph them. Shortly after this, I learned with deep sorrow that Anthony Agpaoa died in a coma on January 30, 1982, after suffering a stroke. He was 42. In spite of his unusual healing abilities, this time Tony was not able to heal himself. He suffered tremendous pressure and harassment from those who did not understand his healing ministry; but uppermost in his mind was the good of mankind.

CHAPTER TWELVE
How Psychic Surgery Works

After observing more than a hundred of Tony Agpaoa's operations, all performed with bare hands, I could detect no fraud or trickery whatsoever; nor did my camera catch such aberrations. Many times I witnessed the healer's fingers entering the body of a patient, with praying and chanting accompanying his surgery. I saw blood and tissues removed and thrown into special pails. The effect on the patient was reported to be occasional dizziness or creation of a dreamlike state accompanied by slight pressure during the operation. No pain was reported by any of them. No scars could be identified after the area was swabbed with cotton, in which minimal traces of blood were cleaned from the skin surface. The operation usually lasted about two minutes. I was never able to find any evidence of infection when, several days later, I asked the patients how they felt. Some of them improved within minutes, while others took several days. Still others necessitated repeated psychic surgery to overcome the problem. I remember only a few patients who were quite skeptical and could not be helped. These persons appeared to me, as a psychiatrist, to possess a profound subconscious need not to get well.

In a number of instances, the healers permitted me to place my hands on the body of a patient during an operation and "transmit energy" to him or her. I felt this energy flow through my hands like a strong electrical current. Earlier, one of the psychic surgeons had touched and blessed my hands, my heart, and my forehead. I felt something akin to electricity pass through my skin, as well as my entire mind and body. They asked me to always pray to G-d in order to help people, claiming their healing is of the patient's spirit, obtained through aligning it with G-d.

Prayers, mantras and chants usually accompany the spiritual healing, such as the following: "Oh, Almighty Lord, here I am to witness and feel your hands, the warmth of your love and radiance of your power. Shower me with your love and mercy, that this operation which I am to receive will be successful, that

I may live longer and continue serving my loved ones and those who need me. Through your precious hands, I submit therefore, myself, with the hopes that I may find for myself a rejuvenation that would help me to carry on my existence in this cosmic world. I trust in you, my dear Lord . . . and so, Thy will be done . . ."

The sacred Sanskrit mantra is then chanted: *baba nam, baba nam, kevallam, param pita baba ki.* ("Attribute everything to G-d and victory is a sure guarantee.")

Reverend Sonny, one of the Philippine psychic surgeons, explained healing as spiritual energy transmitted from the point of the surgical opening to the spiritual center of the individual, after which the energy travels throughout the entire body, healing it. The healer is usually able to locate the problem area by passing his hands over the patient's body. Some acupuncture meridians can also be followed in the process. Regardless of the site of entry into the body, the so-called "laser beam" is emitted by the healer during a meditative raising of vibrations through his hands into the physical body of the healee as the sick tissue is ejected. The healing energy sent by the healer circulates throughout the body, reaches the spiritual center of the individual, and effects the healing.

As a matter of fact, Tony and his crew of healers do not consider themselves psychic surgeons or faith healers, but spiritual healers. Healing is achieved many times in this way without even the need of faith by the healee. Spiritual healers, however, claim the necessity of a prolonged discipline and training for psychic surgery to effect healing. As a matter of fact, they stress the healing is not effected by them; they are merely channels through which the spiritual energy from G-d is directed to the patient. As indicated in their mantra, everything is attributed to G-d. Only then is victory assured.

My own method includes a modified hypnotic technique in which I become meditatively attuned to the Higher Self or G-d within. I do not "enter" the physical body. Entering the physical body is not only illegal in the United States, but is also unnecessary, as the healing can be performed within the thinner form of energy vibration, which is the astral body surrounding the physical body. After a time interval varying from seconds to several days or weeks, the healing spreads into the thicker form of energy vibration - the physical body, and the healing is completed.

I asked several psychic surgeons why they choose to open the physical body and materialize tissues and blood. They responded that the majority of the people who undergo these operations pay a great deal of money to travel to the Philippines. The donations they make to the healers are not their largest expense, and they obviously expect the unusual. Therefore, the body is sometimes opened or sick tissues materialized in the astral body of the patient by raising the energy vibration of these tissues, then rematerializing them by again lowering their level of vibration. No scar is left, as no cells have been cut. The energy vibration of the molecules between the rims of the physical opening has been temporarily raised to permit the fingers and hands to enter.

It is common knowledge that many karate fighters can break a block of bricks with their bare hand after prolonged and disciplined training. In essence, what they do is create a sharp edge of energy along the ulnar aspect of their hand. This energy, like a laser beam, is actually responsible for breaking the bricks. Any physician would testify that the speed with which the hand hits the bricks is easily sufficient to fracture the hand bones. The reason why there are no fractures is due to the special concentration of the fighter. To the unknowing observer, it appears that the hand alone breaks the block of bricks, which is untrue.

In the same way, psychic surgery is accomplished without making contact with the physical body. It works only through the astral body. In many of my own hearings, I used this knowledge to modify my hypnotic technique. Thus, through experience and study, I have found that hypnosis is a *process consisting of different levels of unconsciousness (or subconsciousness)*.

According to the Philippine surgeons, the fourth category of healing is mystical healing. In this form of healing, the healer rejuvenates the body cells by attuning his vibrations to his cosmic source. He does this by charging them with a subtle electromagnetic energy that emanates from his fingers that are, in turn, directed by his mind or consciousness. The belief is held that each of the seven bodies or layers composing man obeys certain laws within its individual plane of existence.

When these layers are not attuned to each other or out of balance, illness results in the physical body, the densest of the layers. Balancing and attuning the other layers results in rejuvenation of the cells; healing is the secondary result of the process.

Divine healing is the fifth category of healing. It can only be accomplished by a highly evolved being. The greatest example of this type of healer is, of course, Jesus Christ. Licauco adds that "cures made through divine healing are always instantaneous, unlike other forms of healing which are generally more gradual."

It is unfortunate that the stringent orthodoxy of the medical profession prevents it from admitting that faith healing can really effect a cure. When a cure through faith healing is demonstrated to them, physicians generally attribute it to one or a combination of the following causes:

1. Wrong diagnosis.
2. The illness is psychosomatic in origin.
3. There has been a spontaneous remission of illness; in other words, the disease would have cured itself even if nothing had been done.

CHAPTER THIRTEEN
The Philosophy of Self Help

In my long experience with hypnosis I have reached the conclusion that it spans varying degrees of unconsciousness — a condition ranging from wakefulness to the profoundest of sleep. It would be not be too far-fetched of me to state that nine out of ten persons are "unconscious" most of their waking hours. Why? Because the subconscious is permitted by the conscious mind to be in charge.

Let us re-examine the levels of consciousness we have been discussing:

LEVELS OF CONSCIOUSNESS	DESCRIPTION
HIGHER SELF OR SUPERCONSCIOUS (G-D WITHIN)	Divine Aspect of Man Source of Conscious Spiritual or Superior Intuition Divine or Unconditional Love and All Other Positive Attributes
MIDDLE SELF OR CONSCIOUS (SOUL)	Intellect, Reasoning and Will Power Potential for Divine Unconditional Love and All Other Positive Attributes World Orientation or Glorification
LOWER SELF OR SUBCONSCIOUS (ANIMAL SPIRIT)	Programmed to Master the Physical Body Memory Bank Source of Emotions and Desires Psyche or Intuition Forms Conditioned Reflexes Automatic Skills and Habits Limited Reasoning

These levels of consciousness are not new. The Lemurians and the Atlanteans, according to several sources, knew them and utilized them to master life. Inca Indians, deriving from an ancient civilization, probably Lemurian, prophesied the same knowledge, symbolically expressed through their Totem Pole, which usually presents three levels: at the bottom, a ferocious animal; in the middle, two people standing on the animal; and on the top, a large "all-seeing" bird with many eyes. Being interested in Hebrew numerology (*Geamatria*), used particularly by Kabbalists, I discovered several years ago during my meditations, to my amazement, that the word "I" in Hebrew "ANY" contains a much deeper meaning than it appears on the surface. Letters in Hebrew stand for numbers too. Therefore, in the word "ANY" ("I"), "A" stands for 1, "N" stands for 50, and "Y" stands for 10. Added up, 1 + 50 + 10 = 61; 6 + 1 = 7. Seven is considered the sacred number (the day G-d rested; the colors of the spectrum; the days of the week; the seven chakras in Yoga philosophy; the openings in the head, etc.) Moreover, if printed vertically, like a totem pole "ANY" looks: ᴬₙʸ

In Hebrew "A" is the first letter of the word "Alef," which means ox or animal, in other words the animal spirit or the Subconscious. The letters in the word "Alef" stand respectively for 1 + 30 + 0 + 80. Added up the total is 111. 1 + 1 + 1 = 3. Three falls short of seven which is the sacred number. Therefore, the animal spirit does not measure up to the sacred level of G-d. "N" in the "letter" totem pole is the first letter of the word *Nefesh*, which translates "soul," the human spirit, or the conscious mind; the respective numbers: 50 + 0 + 80 + 0 + 300 + 0 = 430. 4 + 3 + 0 = 7. This shows the human spirit has the potential to measure up to G-d's level, and that is because man was made in G-d's image. "Y" stands for 10 which by itself is a perfect number, and comes from the word *Adonai* or *Elohim* which means G-d, "Elohim" contains letters which stand respectively for I + 30 + 0 + 5 + 10 + 40 = 86. 8 + 6 = 14. 14 divided by two (male and female counterparts) equals seven, - and again, the number of perfection, the number which symbolizes G-d.

In my chart of the levels of consciousness, the subconscious is programmed to control the physical body. Conscious thought cannot make hair grow. The subconscious also digests food, controls our breathing, administers our elimination and sexual functions, oversees our health and illnesses.

The subconscious contains our memory bank. The memory bank, like a tape recorder, records everything that happens to us - awake or asleep. For instance, we may be asleep and "hear" an argument in the next room. We wake up and react to it, though consciously there has been no awareness of the incident. Still again, negative remarks may be passed along by a surgical staff while a patient is under an anesthetic. Patients have been found to react later to such remarks in a way that proved detrimental to the patient's condition.

As the source of emotions, the subconscious contains our hate, anxiety, anger, depression, and other feelings. Love is not an emotion, but comes from the Superconscious or Higher Self. Personal love, however, is an emotional attachment, and the subconscious retains desire as expressed by sight, sound, touch, smell and taste.

The subconscious is also the source of the psyche or intuition, the so-called sixth sense, or extrasensory perception and other psi abilities. Conditioned reflexes, automatic skills and habits are also at the level of the subconscious. These are positive or negative, according to those circumstances that programmed the subconscious through repetition of pleasant or traumatic experiences. Biases, prejudices, false beliefs, false pride, false principles can be found here. Finally, the subconscious has a limited independent reasoning of its own similar to the mentality of a young child. In our present society, this is about three and one quarter years ranging from two to five and one half, with a maximum of seven. This age is attained by only a few exalted souls, such as Jesus, Moses or Buddha.

The conscious mind or soul of man has reasoning, intellect and will power as its attributes. The superconscious or Higher Self is the divine part of man. G-d is everywhere and is within us as well. Here is the source of spiritual conscience and superior intuition, not to be confused with the lower or psychic intuition of the subconscious.

The reader is referred to the introductory chapter of this book, in which was briefly outlined a holistic philosophy of therapy. Let us now review this subject, which we may conveniently call *the philosophy of self-help through positive mental attitude.*

After more than three decades of experience in therapeutic hypnosis, I have discovered two basic factors in mental and physical well-being — self help and a positive mental attitude. For anything to be a success, it must be developed through hard work. There is no easy way to good health.

The subconscious is a creature of habit, and it learns through motivation and repetition programming. Take as an example the way we learn to write the letters of the alphabet. Through conscious effort and repetition the subconscious learns how to write "A" and "B" and "C." After a time the subconscious attains this skill and performs it automatically. The same is true in learning to drive a car. In the beginning conscious effort and repetition are necessary in order to learn coordination of steering, shifting, observation, and so forth; but after a month or two the subconscious is driving automatically, while the conscious mind pays minimal attention to the road.

Health as well is a skill to be acquired by the subconscious in the same manner. Here motivation is vitally important. Formerly our subconscious possessed positive health skills and habits, but through negative repetition programming and negative emotional experience it lost much of its normal skills and habits. As a result of much negative stimuli throughout our everyday existence, the subconscious cannot help but react negatively sooner or later. Thus, we experience lack of affection during childhood, punitive parents, teachers, and bosses; financial distress; failure in social adjustment; and other results from the conscious mind placing impossible demands on the subconscious. By the same token, if one can consciously bombard the subconscious with repetitious, positive experiences, sooner or later the subconscious will feed back positively.

The subconscious can only be motivated and encouraged to participate in a self-help program after its inner conflicts have been resolved. Once the conflict is uncovered (and this is often found to have its roots in a past life), the problem seems to dissolve. No repetitive reprogramming is necessary. It is important to remain conscious of the discovery and instill enough motivation to the subconscious to change or maintain its new condition. Likewise, after any form of healing, self-help through conscious awareness will generally always result in improvement; nevertheless, nearly half the hearings require some form of repetition programming, since the subconscious appears to be so addicted to the problem that only persistent reprogramming will help. Thus we can state quite categorically that any type of healing depends upon a continuous conscious awareness, both during and after the healing process. However, if a conflict which stems from this or a previous life is not solved, there is a greater possibility for relapse. Therefore, the subconscious (which is estimated to be three and a quarter years of age in mentality) *should be carefully assessed for its age level and approached according to its needs and abilities and limitations.* Generally, the more consciously aware a person is, the older the subconscious; hence, the prospects for consciously promoting, obtaining, and maintaining health are brighter. In addition, the need of repetition programming of the subconscious after conflict disclosure, or even healing, will diminish accordingly. Therefore, health is directly proportionate to the level of conscious and subconscious growth.

By the same token, the need for repetition programming is inversely proportional to the level of conscious awareness. In practice, however, things are not that simple. The subconscious ages of three and four and one-half are the most unstable in manifestation, as this is a period of transition between being predominately ruled by the subconscious and then by the conscious mind. The skill of the therapist should concentrate mainly on enhancing conditions for the individual to become more conscious; hence, one should exercise more self-help and positive mental attitudes through conscious awareness and will. In a subconscious age of less than three years, repetition programming by the therapist appears necessary and self-help and positive mental attitude are generally limited. Between three and three and one-half years of age, the subconscious responds well to both repetition programming by the therapist and/or one's conscious mind. There is, however, a danger of regression to a much younger age of the subconscious. This can mean a serious physical condition or psychosis (i.e., a split between the subconscious and conscious mind) with the result that the subconscious takes over entirely. Since the therapist may tend to rely too heavily on the patient to help himself, the latter may become too regressed and under stress, and fail to measure up to expectations. In most cases, psychosis results because of a forced conscious awareness on a young subconscious (under three years old). Hence, a watchful eye should be kept on such an individual. "Coaching" him into conscious awakening should be prolonged, while more direct repetition programming by the therapist is suggested. This is the type of individual who may, though rarely, commit suicide if not properly supervised.

A great many cases, diagnosed as Manic Depressive Illness, characterized by alternating bouts of depression and hypomanic behavior, start during this age range of the subconscious. They become particularly prevalent during the peak of instability of the subconscious, which occurs between two and three-quarters and four and one-half years of age. At this time, the shifts between subconscious and conscious awareness are wide, quick and frequent.

We can make an interesting and helpful comparison between up to three-and-one-half year old subconscious "TH" and an older subconscious "F" (three-and-one-half to four-and-one-half years old) exposed to excessive conscious awakening. In extreme cases of internally and/or externally applied stress upon the subconscious, the subconscious either attempts to liberate itself by destroying the physical body (heart attack, stroke, cancer, etc.) or by separating from the conscious mind which puts intolerable demands upon it. This last possibility means a psychotic breakdown; this usually happens when a very young subconscious — under three — Is put under undue strain by forced and excessive conscious growth. It is laudable how science lately discovered that the left hemisphere of the brain is primarily concerned with verbal, analytical thinking, while the right is in charge of symbolical, synthetic, emotional and artistic pursuits. Essentially, there is a connection between the two through nerve tissue fibers. Through these fibers, communication is maintained between the two hemispheres. The subconscious seems to work mainly through the right hemisphere, and the conscious mind through the left.

In the age category, "TH" of the subconscious, it is easier to retreat to a younger age category, with possible subsequent detachment of the subconscious from the conscious, as the conscious mind becomes insufficiently manifest to control the subconscious; therefore, the subconscious, with its limited reasoning and unduly delegated power, decides to break away from the conscious mind, resulting in a psychotic breakdown, or a very serious physical condition. It is even possible for the category "F" subconscious to regress to this level but very rarely, and under extraordinary life adjustment pressures. The best diagnosis is made, many times, by giving the person equal opportunities of expression. Category "F" subconscious, when compared with "TH," has a more manifest consciousness which assumes more power over the subconscious, leaving the latter with no chance to misuse its limited reasoning. As a result, the person does not break down psychotically, does not commit suicide, and does not contract a serious physical illness. It is true that the instability that results is quite high in an "F" subconscious. This has to do with wide swings of mood and unhappiness, but assistance in balancing one's moods should not be done indiscriminately (by treatment with Lithium Carbonate, as many physicians do), based on biochemical explanations. First the individual should be enabled to increase his or her consciousness. Becoming more *conscious will result in stability and ultimately in health.*

In an article entitled "A Scan for Mental Illness," (*Discovery Magazine,* October, 1980), Dylan Landis discussed a device called PETT III, which identities manic-depressives and schizophrenics through brain patterns. FDG, a radioactively-tagged, glucose-like substance, is injected intravenously 30 minutes prior to the brain scanning of the patient. Characteristic patterns were found in scans for normal, manic-depressive, and schizophrenic subjects. What is quite impressive is that no connection could be found in the contrast substance between the two hemispheres of the brain in the schizophrenics. In the manic-depressives there was still a connection, though the contrast substance is reduced. In the normal connection between the two hemispheres, ample contrast substance appears well absorbed in the brain.[39]

These scans seem to confirm one of the Huna convictions that in cases of insanity there is a split between the subconscious and conscious mind, and the subconscious mind takes over. (See Figures No. 20-23.) Such a split may be physically induced.

In any case, schizophrenia seems to have an astral cause,

129

Fig. No. 20

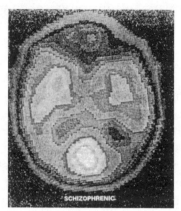

Fig. No. 21

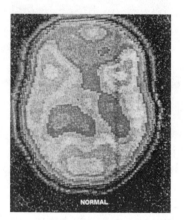

Fig. No. 22

Fig. No. 23

Dr. Tibor Farkas (left) and a technician demonstrate how a patient is readied for a brain scan. The three scans above were made at Brookhaven, and show differences among normal, manic-depressive, and schizophrenic brains.

and healing the astral body may help such a patient to recover. In many instances, such healing is hard to accomplish, and anti-psychotic medication may be used in the overall holistic approach. Biochemical theory indicates that one of the extremities of two nerve connections called postsynaptic end contains receptors that are either overly sensitive to certain biogenic substances (neurotransmitters) produced in the brain, or these substances are produced in excess. Therefore, the remedy seems to be to block the above receptors with chemicals which have proved effective in controlled studies. Reinstating connection between the subconscious and the conscious mind, whether known or not by physicians, seems to be the main objective of the treatment. Following is an example of how a severely disturbed schizophrenic patient can be helped with a nearly, complete absence of anti-psychotic medication.

Laurie was a pretty, 18-year-old girl who had been admitted to the mental unit of a suburban Chicago hospital because of agitated behavior, detachment from reality, physical violence towards her family and insomnia. Her mother and her father had been unable to handle her at home any longer, and had thus sought outside help.

Laurie had been admitted to the hospital by a psychiatrist, who had diagnosed her as having schizophrenic disorder with strong affective counterparts. She was treated by him, according to orthodox psychiatric practice, with anti psychotic medications and mood stabilizers. After a number of large doses of Prolixin, Thorazine, Haldol, and other drugs, as well as mood stabilizers such as lithium carbonate over a period of more than two months, Laurie's condition not only did not improve, but worsened. She became increasingly agitated. The therapy was not reaching her. Laurie was turning out to be one of the unit's most difficult patients in the many years of its existence. Laurie would tease and attack other patients, defecate on the floor, and attempt to hurt herself to the point where the psychiatrist found it necessary to place her in restraints numerous times.

Discussing this difficult case in a unit meeting with other psychiatrists and staff members, approval was received to administer electroshock therapy to Laurie as a last resort. Faced with this alternative, Laurie and her family approached me and requested that I attempt an alternative holistic treatment of

131

Laurie.

When Laurie was transferred to me, I immediately discontinued all of the anti-psychotic drugs and the lithium carbonate, with the exception of a small dose of thorazine, only to be given on an as-needed basis. I then put her on large doses of vitamins — B Complex, C, E, and niacin, in addition to vitamin B-12 injections. She was encouraged to eat nutritious foods, including vegetables and fruits, to drink plenty of water and to refrain from artificial sweets. Also, through a hypnotic technique which influenced her aura consciousness, I assisted her to come in touch with reality as her psychosis cleared and to maintain her state of health. Within two weeks, and to the amazement of the hospital staff, Laurie improved dramatically. Her normal self began to come to the surface — an intelligent, charming and joyful girl.

One might think I performed magic, but this was not the case. I simply based my treatment on universally proven laws which I had learned through my clinical testing of hypnosis. This included many ideas and techniques of psychic healing, sound nutrition and physical exercise.

Laurie was discharged from the hospital upon being instructed as to how to help herself and that I should always be available should she need me in the future. She left on her own for Missouri, where she was accepted by one of the colleges there.

A year later Laurie called me and told me that since her discharge from the hospital, she had been healthy and happy and progressing with her studies. She said she felt like a new person altogether, and no longer used drugs of any kind.

Between the ages four-and-a-half and seven of the subconscious, the conscious mind exerts strong control over our destiny. Illness is a rare and short-lived occurrence, and only then when one temporarily slips back from one's conscious training. An individual with this subconscious maturity is usually *always* healthy; repetition programming is minimal or not necessary at all. Conscious insight into problems is usually enough to make the subconscious respond accordingly. Such individuals make the easiest patients, as they well understand the value of staying conscious and utilizing self help and positive mental attitude. They usually can heal themselves.

In regards to positive mental attitude: what you think, you create; what you feel, you attract; and what you imagine, you sooner or later become — usually through repetition. Thoughts have power, for they possess a transparent form of energy that cannot be seen by the naked eye. (The reader is referred to Figure 9, where electrophotographs of telepathic thoughts are illustrated.) Previously we noted that should one build a negative mold of a thought and fill it with negative emotions, anger, fear, worry, etc., sooner or later that thought is going to translate itself into negative action. By the same token, should one build a positive mold of a thought and fill it with positive emotions and enthusiasm, the opposite will occur.

Let us now return to the idea of self help. Although most people scrupulously look after their house, car, and job, they take their health for granted. *Attaining "health consciousness" means patient, persistent, and consistent self-help, knowing oneself, and repetition programming and utilizing positive mental attitude.* But most people lack patience, and after putting the seed in the ground, they start to scratch the earth every day to see if it is growing, rather than watering it and patiently waiting until a beautiful flower appears.

Following is an affirmation used by Rosita Rodriguez and myself which has proved successful with many of my patients:

"This is the first day of the rest of my life, and I shall live it in good health and abundance, using every moment of it, doing the constructive, positive things I want to, and surrounding myself with people of my choice, in pursuit of love, peace and joy.

"Every day and every night, I am becoming more consciously aware of myself, and the world surrounding me. It feels so good; it feels so good!"

Success and communication are two elements not fully understood. Success research demonstrates that only 15 percent of success can be attributed to knowledge; 85 percent is the result of the human factor. Studies in communication reveal that only 7 percent of our communication is verbal, with the remainder nonverbal. It has to do with the way one comes across through images, emotions, actions, personal example, tone of voice, and so forth. Such findings are not surprising when we realize that most people are unconscious most of the time; their subconscious has an average age of three and a quarter years. In other words, the subconscious acts like a three and a quarter-year-old child. Children that age understand better in pictures than words, and the actions and the convincing tone of voice are additionally important. Thus we can say, consciously communicating with your own subconscious is not much different than communicating with somebody else's subconscious; therefore, the above affirmation will not be enough to establish full communication with your subconscious. You will have to translate the words into pictures, present them to the eyes of your mind, and put them across with conviction, kindly but firmly as you would do with a young child. Thus, when you read: "This is the first day of the rest of my life," you should enthusiastically visualize a beautiful day. The sun is bright and the sky blue. You feel consciously this is to be a new start in your life. You keep visualizing yourself in that background, radiating a bright white glow of wholeness, health, energy and happiness. As you visualize these feelings, inhale deeply three times, feeling the energy entering your head and staying there. By doing so more nutrients are burned in your body and the energy derived through this process makes your thought-picture creations sink better into your subconscious.

Since the subconscious has the mentality of a young child, the notion of time is vague to it. It has the notion of timelessness; time is forever. In this respect then, one may visualize the light of day, the dark of night, the light of day, the dark of night, etc. This sequence the subconscious may understand means "all the time." In other words, whatever is to be accomplished is not only for now, but all the time, for all the time, continuously. "Doing the constructive, positive things I want to. . ." This can be visualized on your mind screen, literally doing the constructive positive things you want to, whether it is with your family, professionally, socially, or in some other activity.

"Surrounding myself with people of my choice." Here, , visualization has to do with conscious choice of people, "In pursuit of love, peace, and joy." One can envision here love as bright white light spilling from oneself all over the world; peace of mind experienced while lying on green grass seen with the mind's eye; and joy would be enjoying the beauty of creation on a spiritual level, while on a worldly level enjoying your spouse, or partner, or even making love, which you and your dear one enjoy to its fullest.

As we well know, give to G-d what belongs to G-d, and to Caesar what belongs to Caesar. But, what is amazing, is that every time you bring to the screen of your mind the picture of another person besides the one of yourself, you already communicate with the subconscious of that person. That is why many times people with sexual dysfunction can be helped through this repetitious mental exercise. "Every day and every night I am becoming more consciously aware of myself and the world surrounding me, and it feels so good, it feels so good!" This last sentence speaks for itself. It is so important to become and stay as conscious as possible.. This is true not only during the day, but during the night too, when the level of unconsciousness is more pronounced than during the day. Therefore, it is a good idea to be in conscious control during the night, since, for example, most heart attacks occur during the night. You may stop them this way and not let prevail the limited reasoning of the subconscious which wants "to check out" for some unknown reason to you.

In addition, you may become consciously aware of your breathing, the way you look or dress, a tree, or a sign you did not see before on the street, etc. The main point to put across to the subconscious is the idea of your becoming more and more conscious and in charge, so that the subconscious will get used to it. You can now see how a simple and rational affirmation can be properly and consciously communicated to the subconscious. And remember, visualization is important. The ancient Chinese proverb: "A picture is worth a thousand words," is not without merit.

I should remind the reader that one of the major mistakes a person often makes is to regard himself as a single entity. The fact that too often the individual views himself as "one piece," is the root of most of our problems. As I stressed previously, besides the physical body, a person has a double body. The aura-consciousness, made of a thinner form of energy vibration than the physical body, can be at least partly photographed with our present day technological advancement in Kirlian photography. In this way, a brilliant, beautiful, colorful crown is obtained around living things. Not only that, but it has been emphasized before how this consciousness survives after the physical body's ablation, or death. Thus, up to now, at least two components were found in one person, the physical body and consciousness. But consciousness contains three important levels: the superconscious or Higher Self; the conscious mind, the Middle Self or Soul of man; and the subconscious, the Lower Self or animal spirit. These levels of consciousness may be labeled as spirits, entities, levels of energy vibration. But no matter how they are labeled, they stand for the same thing, having the same significance and qualities. The reader is referred back to the chart which shows the "Levels of Consciousness," to assist in understanding what is to follow.

CHAPTER FOURTEEN
The Bible and Its Mystery

Any thoughtful study of history will tell us that the consciousness of man is constantly evolving. Truths that were hidden from the masses centuries ago for fear of misunderstanding and misuse, are accepted quite readily today. Earlier attitudes toward our own physical universe offer a good example. The sixteenth century took a far different view of science than does the twentieth. Rather than suffer condemnation as they did in the sixteenth century, Bruno and Galileo would no doubt today share the Nobel Prize!

It was perhaps because of such an unevolved consciousness existing in the past that the Bible was written in a secret code.

Its more esoteric, spiritual meanings were available to the few who could understand and use them for their own development, but the vast majority were kept ignorant of the truth. They were not ready to *know* consciously, though they could be made to *believe* subconsciously.

My research into the various levels of the subconscious has convinced me that the Bible can be interpreted by different ages of the subconscious in various ways. Each subconscious level will find an interpretation suitable to its capacity. After all, when the subconscious is very young, it will quite naturally look for someone with an old subconscious for guidance. Thus, as the subconscious grows in age, old interpretations of the Bible will make sense no longer; deeper meanings will be sought.

Another reason, as we suggested earlier, why the Bible is written in secret code is to hide from the ignorant and the powerful knowledge which they might well abuse. For example, the acceptance by the masses of Jesus as the Son of G-d through whom they will reach G-d, would pose no threat to the powerful, to the oppressors of the masses. But one might assume that if the eyes of the masses were to be opened by a teacher such as Jesus, where the son stands symbolically for the Soul or conscious mind of each individual through which one can reach G-d or superconsciousness within himself, then the individual would have as much power as his oppressor. It would be difficult to maintain control over the masses any longer.

From a study of various source materials, one cannot but conclude that Jesus was well informed about reincarnation. Schooled for nearly twenty years in different lands of the East, he became an apt pupil of healing and the doctrine of rebirth. Unfortunately, the Council of Constantinople declared reincarnation to be a heresy in A.D. 381, and the masses continued to be the victims of their own ignorance.

In the Kabbala, the esoteric Judaic interpretation of the Scriptures, we find reference to reincarnation. But with the interventions of Constantine and Theodora in the fourth century, serious deletions were made in the Bible which have not been restored. However, we do find much of this material in *The Aquarian Gospel of Jesus the Christ by* Levi, in which the missing years of Jesus' life are made known. Here we also find explained that Christ signifies Divine Love. It is this that Jesus really represents, and it is the same Divine Love which all of us can achieve through conscious awareness of our own divine heritage, our union with G-d.

In the story of creation, the Bible presented, again in secret code, events predating Jesus. Man is presented as the real creator who fell into ignorance, who forgot his divine origin. Time — and this is being supported more and more by modern science — is a creation of man in order that the subconscious can experience its earthly existence. Hence, creation is not a fact of the past, but a continuous process. Though the subconscious cannot apprehend it as such, the universe is infinite. Only the higher soul can understand this.

The universe, including ourselves, is in a constant, continuing state of movement; therefore, it is impossible for us to project a beginning or an end to space. This can be acceptable to the conscious mind, but the subconscious is forever attracting itself to the finite. It is for this reason that so many people see life as a final destination rather than a journey, because they permit the subconscious to rule them.

One question that might arise is: Why does G-d create so many inferior types of energy vibration rather than those equivalent to his own highest vibration? The answer is that there seems to be continuous movement in creating gradients of energy vibration; if this movement were to stop, and all energy vibrations assume those of the nature of G-d, then G-d or the universe would disappear. If such a phenomenon could be arranged, at least on a small scale, this would mean finding ourselves somewhere else in the universe, perhaps billions of light-years away from the initial point. By lowering vibrations, we would materialize again and again, become engaged in the continuous movement which is the essence of the existence of G-d's infinite universe. Perhaps this explains how living creatures from other galaxies, where physical life as we know it on earth is conceivable, may appear in our skies as UFOs by raising their spaceship's and their own vibrations temporarily. Tungsten carbide, which was discovered by two Swedes in the 1950's, close to the UFOs they claim to have witnessed, was analyzed and found not to be comparable to any mineral on earth.

It is interesting to speculate if these Tungsten carbide crystals are so constituted that through contraction and dilation the level of energy vibration of the spaceship is increased or decreased, thereby overcoming certain lines of magnetism in the universe. Might not this result in projecting the spaceship, possibly billions of light-years away, to a place in the universe suitable to the decreased energy vibration to which the spaceship must return in order to abide by the Law of Continuous Movement? Perhaps this explains why UFOs are reported as appearing and disappearing so quickly. In other words, are they decreasing and then increasing their energy vibration? It would appear so.

As an extension of G-d, man is a little G-d — but he does not know it. Knowing is better than believing, however, knowing takes place at the level of the conscious mind. Everything in this universe is an extension of G-d, from the lowest to the highest form of energy vibration, and *every form of energy vibration has the potential to join the highest*. After achieving this, man must return to the initial level or another entity will go to that lower energy vibration to preserve an adequate gradient of energy; therefore, we have the Universal Law of Continuous Movement, expansion and contraction, which is the essence of existence in G-d's infinite universe. We can now readily see that self-help and positive mental attitude

139

are the keys to health, happiness, and good interpersonal relationships. The unified Soul-G-d is now seen as self-sufficient and unlimited in power; being able to effect the self-help, it also views this union as the only one able to create positively, because G-d is only good; therefore, he is capable of only positive mental attitude. But Jesus, the man, lost his life on earth when he taught the truth, no matter how disguised it might have been.

G-d gave man the potential to choose between the highest and lowest forms of energy vibration. This is the meaning behind the tree of good and evil. Through its will, the Soul is endowed with a potential to choose. The Soul- Spirit chose to come on earth and share the physical body of the animal with the animal spirit-the subconscious. Adam and Eve symbolize the male and female counterparts; because of that, the Soul was made in their image.

I discovered many years ago that in the Hebrew language (which has numbers for each letter) FATHER AND MOTHER = CHILD (AV + EIM = IELED). At that time it merely drew my interest;' but now it makes sense symbolically, in view of how G-d, with its male and female counterparts, created the Soul the "child" in its own image. This polarity is another expression of Continuous Movement as a universal law. It is a reminder of our potential power to recreate ourselves into a higher form of energy vibration, by the same token that an animal cell has the ability to reproduce an entire body through cloning.

It seems more difficult for the subconscious to jump directly to the highest form of energy vibration — which is G-d, and unite with It. It may never do so. Only the Soul of man can do this; otherwise, the Universal Law of Continuous Movement will be upset, which cannot happen absolutely, but only relatively. Under these circumstances, Einstein's theory of relativity, $E = MC^2$, becomes obsolete in the infinite universe with the Continuous Movement Law, as it takes into account time, a subconscious notion. The formula may therefore be changed to reflect this universal, infinite truth rather than a limited truth. Therefore, the above formula will become $E = MC \infty$. In essence, it will mean that $E = M$, or energy equals matter. This implies that energy can be transformed into matter, and inversely, that matter is a form of energy and energy a form of matter. In other words, what we call matter is relative, for it is at the same time energy; what we call energy is really relative as it is also matter.

In any case, Adam and Eve symbolically represent the soul of man, later to be expelled from the Garden of Eden or G-d; not literally, of course, but by a relative loss of awareness of itself. This happened simply through directing the subconscious to run its experience on earth, by lowering its energy vibration to the level of the subconscious. How? By switching from Christ to Anti-Christ — the fundamental world polarity found in each individual or group of individuals at certain varying rates — is like a universal sisa, tilting forever, in order to achieve karmic balance. This "tilting" is eternal and conforms with the fundamental universal Law of Continuous Movement. The only salvation for the Soul is to be resurrected once and for all. Once It is reunited with G-d's highest vibration, it may always remain at that level.

Avatars offer an example to mankind in how to separate from the animal spirit (resurrect), and return to the Lost Paradise — how to be back with G-d, as man and woman created in his/ her image.

Most prayers go unanswered because they are addressed to a third entity — G-d, but they end at the animal spirit (or subconscious) level; the animal does not know what to do with them or is simply willful like a little child and stubbornly refuses to comply with them. The truth of the matter is, if logically we are as souls made in G-d's image the same level of energy vibration — then we are already one with G-d. Therefore, what is the point of addressing G-d as a third entity? The kingdom of G-d is within and everywhere. That is why the *effective prayer* is as Jesus taught it to his disciples on the Mount of Olives. He advised his disciples to pray on the mountain and in the closet of their souls. In this way the prayer will be heard. In other words, *manifest the positive attributes of G-d* (be on the "mountain"—be this way with G-d), positive thinking and *do it — self-help*. You do not pray to a young child playing with matches to stop playing with them. You must take the matches, explain the danger, and give him a teddy bear instead. This child continues to be happy, but safely this time according to your superior reason, rather than the, limited reasoning of the child — that could have set both of you on fire! There are many such situations when one may deprogram the subconscious of negatives and reprogram it positively. That means taking dominion over the animal or giving to Caesar what belongs to Caesar and to G-d what belongs to G-d. You the soul — the conscious *do it* — make the animal spirit change positively and this is self help.

Knowing and not doing is yet not knowing is a Zen precept, which also is referred to in the Bible in different chapters. But it is most obvious in John 16, and Matthew 5-7 (The Sermon on the Mount).

Logically any positive attribute is a divine attribute. Positive thinking or a soul manifesting the positive attributes of G-d (divine love, wisdom, joy, freedom, peace, truth, etc.) means elevating one's energy vibration to the highest and being again united with G-d (in the above Bible chapters symbolically being on the mount). Each avatar appears to represent a specific G-dly attribute: Jesus — Divine Love; Moses — Freedom; Buddha-Wisdom; Krishna — Joy.

Relaxation is of paramount importance to promote positive thinking and self help. Through relaxation one becomes a good conductor for higher energy which then is channeled to transform a static reaction ("blueprint," or image) into a moving reality. During the seventh day, after six days of creation, G-d rested. This means that rest or relaxation is essential in order to make the creation manifest. The number seven is again symbolical and it emphasizes as the perfect or G-dly number the fundamental importance of relaxation in order to translate any static creation into a moving reality. Therefore, as man was created in G-d's image, he is to create the same way. But "rest" or relaxation has a deeper meaning than Sabbath or Sunday and it means we must constantly relax in order to further our static creations into moving realities. As emphasized before, this should be done through effective prayer. One should be with G-d by constantly manifesting its positive attributes — through *positive thinking*, and make things happen — make for instance the subconscious change in the direction of positivity; all this should be accompanied at all times by *relaxation*. Relaxation enables free movement of the highest energy which activates a moving reality. Biofeedback is an example of empirical conditioning of the subconscious to accomplish exactly that — a higher level of energy vibration (alpha state) corresponding to a deeper level of relaxation. Health energy is a higher energy, too, and it can manifest when one becomes a good conductor through relaxation.

CHAPTER FIFTEEN
The Subconscious

As we observed before, it seems logical that the physical body, as a low form of energy vibration, will respond to its immediately superior form of energy vibration which is the subconscious. The subconscious will then respond to the conscious mind, the conscious mind to the superconscious, and the superconscious to the Universal G-d. In any case, it appears that the conscious mind is grossly unable to direct the subconscious so long as it continues to keep its level of vibration largely in line with the subconscious. Eventually, the subconscious takes over.

No matter how much the subconscious elevates its energy vibration level, (seven years of age in mentality considered the highest) the Universal Law of Continuous Movement prevents it from going higher. At this point in subconscious growth, the conscious mind is back to its highest level of energy vibration, with G-d. It can now separate once and for all from the subconscious. We call this resurrection. Through increased conscious awareness, it is no longer necessary to have a seven-year-old subconscious in order to resurrect one's Soul. Remember, the subconscious cannot resurrect, cannot become one with G-d, as this will be contrary to the Universal Law of Continuous Movement!

Ego is a mixture of mostly lowly subconscious vibrations and the conscious mind, and it vastly overrates itself. Unlike the Animal (subconscious) which kills when hungry, the ego kills just for the sake of killing, for pride, and for power. Most human suffering is a result of the ego. At its highest its mentality may reach twelve years of age. Becoming conscious of our ego is therefore of paramount importance, because only then may we dissolve its negative aspects and eliminate the suffering of ourselves and others.

In the United States we live in a state of affairs in which there is a gradual rise in consciousness; in other words, the conscious mind is slowly returning to its highest vibration. It is beginning to separate from the subconscious. At the same time, the subconscious is raising its energy vibration to its relative maximum

145

rather than seven years of age. That is why the conscious mind has begun questioning more what was before unconsciously accepted. We are questioning certain aspects of our lives, those programmed subconscious computerized schemes that no longer make any sense.

Einstein rightly said: "The important thing is not to stop questioning!" He knew intuitively what he was talking about. With the rise in consciousness in our society, people question more and more. I undertook my own questioning in the form of meditation, which is a method of raising energy vibration to the level of the superconscious. I there received knowledge in the form of an instant realization which I combined with research into others' work and my own clinical experience. I have now decided to share what I found, for the Divine Love which engulfed me prompted me to share it with you, whether it is accepted or not. More and more the conscious mind recognizes the state of misery, unhappiness, illness, and bad interpersonal relationships caused by the subconscious; and the more the realization, the more the increase in conscious awareness.

Before age three of the subconscious, a person will believe nearly anything said by authority, whether it be true or not. The authority can point to a pen and tell the child it is an orange and be believed. The same thing occurs with a normal child before three years of ago. Under three years of age, the subconscious might make a person marry, stay married, have a large family, work in the same occupation as his parents, never move, and be happy with all this. At the same time, the subconscious will witness the conscious mind becoming "a pain in the neck," asking a lot of questions about things previously accepted and believed, becoming more independent, and so forth. This is what is happening in our society, as the subconscious begins to go beyond three. This is why there is turmoil and unhappiness in our society. As a matter of fact, between the ages of three and five, there is a period of accelerated transition from being subconscious to being conscious, only it happens through shifting back and forth, more conscious ground being gained each time. But this shifting back and forth becomes enough to create confusion. It is as if I see the pen as an orange for one moment, and then I see the pen as a pen, until the confusion sets in. Not only that, there are many pens and oranges in our life, enough to confuse us terribly. Under three the subconscious can remain more or less at the same level for millions of years, growing very slowly and generally at the same pace; but now they have grown fast and unequally. Only within two or three generations some of them may reach age seven. Confusion brings about tension and unhappiness, since **one** sees something missing here for the first time. By looking for happiness people are on the right track; the problem is they look for it in the wrong way. Drugs, material goods, and wasted night life will provide them with answers for their problems. We know by now that the subconscious can never be satisfied. It is like a child receiving candy; there is never enough.

If people only knew the right way to happiness they would indeed be happy. This way leads to the Lost Paradise, to the Garden of Eden — back to G-d where the Soul once lived in bliss. *The only real way to happiness is spirituality.* Being spiritual, however, does not necessarily mean being religious, but being consciously related.

A person can start now to become consciously related to his or her physical body, which is the Soul's and the subconscious's vehicle on earth, by realizing the body needs sufficient exercise and rest; in addition, it needs proper nutrition and care in the purchase of food. There are some 5,000 different preservatives and artificially added chemicals in our food products (all approved by the FDA in the United States.) One must consciously relate to the manner of eating and the taste of food. Eating small quantities of food, savoring it in the mouth, thus "relating" to it, makes us eat less and enjoy more; this in turn helps maintain a healthy and esthetically pleasing body.

Consciously relating to the air one breathes is extremely important. That is why clean air free of pollutants is sought by many consciousness-raising environmentalists. Many times I see patients who come to me very anxious and depressed, and what I discover is that they stop breathing for various periods of time; their stomachs do not move. It is usually a society rushing to achieve more and more that is the villain holding one's breath to get to the destination; but then there are many other destinations; there is never an end.

Fear is another reason for the subconscious to hold the abdomen stiff, as though someone were threatening to stick a fist in the solar plexus. One of the major causes of anxiety and depression is when a person is not breathing. Then, when the conscious mind tells the subconscious to breathe, the lungs and diaphragm respond. After four or five deep breaths, the person becomes so relaxed and serene that they may exclaim: "I've never thought about it before, it is all so simple!" Surely it is simple because there is not enough oxygenation in the brain, the switchboard operator through which the subconscious and the conscious mind work. Then the conductivity in these wires becomes hindered due to their impaired metabolism. This results in anxiety, depression, or irritability, which in turn make people argue, overeat, abuse alcohol, take tranquilizers, and so forth. In reality, the solution is simple: breathe deeply several times, and often.

When the subconscious is overtaxed from excessive demands by the conscious mind, it becomes fed up, so to speak, and wants "to check out," often by stopping breathing, or stopping the heart in the middle of the night. In our society, the conscious mind becomes manifest much faster than the subconscious can follow; hence, there is an ever-increasing widening gap between the subconscious and the hardy pace of the conscious mind. The consequence has been stress-ridden lives that often result in heart attacks, cancers, strokes, ulcers, addictions to food, alcohol, cigarettes, television, work, and the like. After all, the conscious mind may make grandiose plans (it has the ability to do so), but someone must carry out those plans. This is that poor animal, the subconscious. After being the recipient of exaggerated demands to which it cannot measure up, the subconscious becomes extremely unhappy. The subconscious, the animal, came into this world to express itself, to enjoy life, and to be happy. No one asked man's spirit — the Soul or conscious entity — to share the body with the animal and make it unhappy. The subconscious is placed under great stress. This is why it may stop the body's breathing, or create a heart attack especially during the night, in order to stop its suffering.

As one becomes more conscious, one starts relating to the subconscious, understanding its needs and abilities, and respecting them. Render unto Caesar what is Caesar's, and render unto G-d what is G-d's. The subconscious may be removed from its cycle of stress by respecting its pace and growth. This is done by giving the subconscious a break now and then, by taking an enjoyable vacation, enjoying a game or play that the subconscious likes. Different exercises that include relaxation and meditation may also take the subconscious off its cycle of stress. Thus, becoming consciously related to your subconscious is not only understandings its needs and abilities, but also supervising it. Thus disciplined, it cannot drag you into mischief or perhaps a fatal accident.

Imagine a three-year-old child playing with matches in your house. Would you let the child do this if you were there? Obviously not. You would take the matches away from him and explain their danger. You might even light a match and bring it close to the skin of his hand, so he can feel the heat. "See, it is hot!" The child will understand and retract his hand. Still, the child knew it had fun playing with matches, and you took them away from him. In order not to frustrate him, you may give him in exchange a teddy bear, a doll, or a toy train. The child may not accept it at first, but he will soon have fun playing with it; it will bring him the same pleasure. The difference is that you, the conscious being, did the reasoning — not the limited reasoning of the subconscious. The child is playing safely now, while before he could have set the house and perhaps himself on fire. By keeping a distance from the child you can prevent him from doing any silly thing; you can relate to him and teach him. This is the way the child or the subconscious learns and matures. In this way it grows older, and the soul — the real self — can grow further into spirituality.

Imagine that instead of consciously relating to the chart with the Levels of Consciousness, I were instead to press my face into it, I would see nothing. I would become "one" with the chart. This is one of the main roots of an individual's unhappiness — when the soul becomes one with the animal, rendering itself blind, as it were, and letting the animal lead. One can expect only misery, suffering, unhappiness, illness, confusion and bad interpersonal relationships by doing so.

Spirituality means to consciously relate to your own subconscious. Only then do you take your rightful position, being the leader rather than the led; this, in turn, brings about happiness to you and your subconscious alike.

CHAPTER SIXTEEN
Growth of Understanding

As you relate to your subconscious, you realize for the first time that most people around you are subconsciously three years old. Would you take to heart the statement of a three-year-old? Certainly not. Knowing this, you should become more tolerant of people, and becoming tolerant will make it easier to smile at them- , And when you smile at the world, the world will usually smile — back. (Remember the song, "When you're smiling, when you're smiling, the whole world smiles with you."?) In this way, your relationships on earth improve, which is good for your Soul growth and for the animal's happiness. Moreover, by exercising conscious control over your subconscious, you are not any longer at the whim of destiny! You are finally, your own master, as you were meant to be in G-d's plan because if you help yourself, G-d will help you too. A film *Oh, G-d!*, released a number of years ago, depicts the protagonist asking the age-old question of G-d: Why do You create us only to have us live in misery, suffering and unhappiness? Why, don't You help us? G-d answered that when he created man he gave him all that it takes to be happy. In other words, he gave him a Soul — he is the Soul — coming from G-d, created in the image of G-d; therefore, man when united with G-d has unlimited power to rule rather than be ruled by the animal self and the animal kingdom. The theme of the movie is relevant to our discussion, for as man becomes more spiritual, more consciously related, he makes the subconscious happier, too.

Walking through a garden is not done in a rush unconsciously, but consciously — relating to the grass you walk on, to the beautiful trees and flowers, smelling their marvelous aroma and relating to them consciously.

Sex is no longer a mechanical, automatic, unconscious process, but is consciously enjoyed to the fullest every, moment.

Driving a car does not any more mean watching only the asphalt in front of you, but also seeing the beautiful trees, along the road, which perhaps you had not noticed before, reveling in the sun shining through the light blue sky, the clouds and rain — seeing them all- as suddenly it dawns upon you that logically it must be a supreme force that created all this beauty. Whether it is called Cosmic Force, Nature, Divine Force, G-d or the Higher Self, it essentially stands for the same thing — the Perfect Creator. Then, for the first time, you consciously come into touch with G-d within you and everywhere. When Moses, Jesus, and other avatars spoke with G-d, they were not unbalanced. They became attuned to their superconscious. It was then the Divine Wisdom, Divine Love, and other supreme attributes of G-d such as positive thinking were unveiled. Reaching G-d within one self, one suddenly receives in a fraction of a second so much enlightenment that formerly difficult problems seem trivial and easy to solve. For the first time one discovers the meaning of life, the purpose on this earth. All of this happiness occurs in a fraction of a second.

What is our purpose here? Are we born just to go unconsciously through life, waking up in the morning, washing our face, eating, engaging ourselves in the same routine work, falling into bed, and waking up the following morning to repeat the cycle? We do have a purpose — to return to the lost paradise-to G-d — where there is eternal bliss and ecstasy. In John, 16:28 of the New Testament we read: "I came forth from the Father, and am come into the world: again, I leave the world, and go to the Father." This verse concerns initiation of the disciples of Jesus and more than any other verse in the Bible reveals how the Soul left its own awareness and G-d's when it decided to descend from Him and live with the animal on Earth; then through a rise in consciousness it found the potential path to Salvation, Resurrection and G-d. Most people are still so bogged down in their subconscious that only very seldom do they relate or come in touch with the Creator, with G-d. It stands to reason that the key is *becoming conscious!* And the highest expression of being conscious is being with G-d, knowing G-d, rather than subconsciously believing in him because some authority preaches it. Being on the mountain or being with G-d, like the avatars, means practically expressing the positive attributes of G-d such as Divine Love, Divine Wisdom, Peace, Joy, Freedom, Power, Health, Wealth, Truth, Harmony, Perfection, Happiness, Bliss, Relaxation and the like;

in other words, positive mental attitude, and not only occasionally but continuously. Because the subconscious is allowed to play such a vital role in our life, learning to understand the subconscious and master it is imperative in the process of becoming conscious. The subconscious must not be required to become a saint or G-d as some fundamentalist religious beliefs aver, nor must it be given all it asks for, like a spoiled child who pays lip service to G-d. Materialism is its very life, and this is encouraged indirectly by other religious beliefs. In both situations the interpretation of the subconscious is wrong, and is not going to work.

The seventh of the Ten Commandments brought forth by Moses from Mount Sinai, with G-d's word, not to commit adultery, had nothing to do with the animal subconscious. G-d knows that the animal cannot measure up to this commandment anyway, because of its limited reasoning; besides it doesn't know how. Therefore, G-d cares less whether two subconsciouses or two bodies sleep with each other, for it knows the animal is not capable of understanding. Hence, that commandment is made for the Soul — the conscious entity — which has the ability to understand it, and it means: "Don't get involved with the animal, betraying me, your G-d; don't commit this adultery against me!" Being the seventh, a sacred number, it symbolizes all the commandments.

It is logical that the only marriage that lasts forever, and never ends in divorce, is the Union of Soul and G-d. It is always good; it is always the best. This is the eternally blissful marriage. Subconsciouses and bodies marry each other, a union officiated over by a priest or rabbi. But this relationship is temporary. It may end in divorce — or persist over several lifetimes, as we know through research. We have learned that about one in five couples were married at least once before in a previous life; still the relationship is relatively short-lived. We come alone into the world and we leave alone.

The marriage that is bliss and ecstasy, and lasts forever, is our marriage to G-d. The Soul should therefore become aware that it did not need, in the-first place, to come on Earth and live with the animal; G-d gave it the choice, the potential, and now after choosing the animal, the Soul can witness the grave mistake it made and choose G-d again, never needing to return to the animal. The animal will be happier, too, as it has all its needs and was happy prior to the Soul's sharing its body. As I mentioned before, the animal who reaches the maximum of seven years of age is not meant to resurrect. Resurrection is only for the Soul which is the highest energy vibration created by G-d. In Genesis: 3:15, G-d admonished the serpent (which symbolizes the subconscious) "... it shall bruise thy head and thou shalt bruise his heel." By this is meant the subconscious animal style of life will be restricted. (What animal for example, works from nine to five and beyond?). Also, the conscious "heel" — the Soul's mobile and infinite intelligence — will be poisoned and in this way limited.

The union of G-d and Soul is the goal. Interestingly enough, in the Hebrew language, ihud means union and it also mean the union with G-d. In Hebrew there are three written forms- of the letter "H." The ancient Hebrews, in order to transform ihud into a sacred name symbolizing union, with G-d, changed the "h" in the word from *het* to *hei*. Het is a Hebrew "h" which is numerically 8, while hei is 5 Due to this change, 1 (10) + H (5) + U (6) + D (4) = 25; 2 + 5 = 7. Seven is the sacred number, the number of completion, the number of perfection. Therefore, any person who belongs to *ihud* - the Union with G-d — is *ihudi*, which translates into "Jewish" in English. Hence, by this definition, any human who has a union with G-d is Jewish. Due to misinterpretation by fundamentalists ihudi (Jewish) was superficially regarded as standing for the name of a nation, religion and culture. The people who were involved in this Union declared themselves the chosen ones.

All people can have union with G-d. But such union with G-d is for the Soul not the animal. Therefore, the animal should not be expected, as is believed by some fundamentalists, to resurrect and become a G-d. This is not possible, for the result will be giving G-d what belongs to Caesar and giving to Caesar what belongs to G-d. Because the animal-Caesar-the subconscious — is not able to measure up to the highest level of G-d's energy vibration, it is going to become frustrated, angry, hostile and homicidal or suicidal.

I teach my students in hypnosis that bringing someone out of a hypnotic trance, which is a deepened state of unconsciousness, should be done gradually with due patience;

otherwise, the patient may become dizzy, or get a headache.

Likewise, the subconscious age level can be *gradually* raised up the limit of seven years of age. Stress in our society is the main result of asking the subconscious to be G-d; or, if not at its highest potential, forcing it to take several steps at a time, rather than a slower course. If we can do this right, virtually most illnesses can be eliminated.

CHAPTER SEVENTEEN
Attributes of the Subconscious

Now let us concentrate on the attributes of the subconscious, because before being able to reach G-d, we should learn to communicate well with the subconscious, be its best friend on Earth. There is a method of guided imagery that helps communicate with the subconscious, and you the conscious mind can converse face-to-face with your subconscious as you would do with another person. This way, after acquainting yourself well with the subconscious, you may come to positive, constructive, and healthy agreements, according to your superior reasoning, rather than the limited reasoning of the subconscious. Remember our story of the three-year-old child playing with matches, and how you may take the matches away, and get the child to agree to play with a safer teddy bear? Well, the subconscious is programmed to control the physical body. It can give us illness or health.

"Very well," somebody will question, "then what about bacteria, viruses, cancerous cells, poisons, genetic factors, accidents, bad personal relationships — aren't these the things that make one sick?" I have no doubt that these are harmful factors, but it takes the agreement of the subconscious before they can exercise their destructive influence on the body and mind. It is the subconscious that gives the green or the red light to these factors to become or not to become harmful. This depends on the limited reasoning of the subconscious — its conflicts, its needs and whether or not the conscious mind exercises enough control over it at the same time. If one examines a slide under a microscope with a secretion from a normal individual, one finds bacteria, cancerous cells, and other abnormal cells. One might wonder how this person is still alive. Simply, because the subconscious by itself, or at the directive of the conscious mind, activates the immune system and other systems of the body, and destroys the harmful factors before they get too far out of hand.

An example of how the subconscious alone or directed by the conscious mind does or doesn't protect against an illness is this: when flu is around, and many people get it, while others don't, most have the virus in their throats. It is simply because the subconscious decided not to have the flu. Perhaps the individual decided he had no time to be sick, there is a lot to do, and a great deal of responsibility to fulfill, and there is simply no time for illness. So the individual does not get sick. By the same token, for example, a couple, both diabetic, parents of ten children, would obviously pass on their genetic predisposition to all their children. Yet only three out of ten may get diabetes. What happened to the other seven? Obviously, they decided not to be sick, while the ones who became sick were identified with the parents. I remember one of my patients, a very young man who, because his father committed suicide, and because he heard that children of parents who commit suicide may end up committing suicide themselves, concluded that he would kill himself. After explaining to him the philosophy of self-help and that he indeed has a choice, he became a new person with a bright outlook on life.

The subconscious is programmed to control the physical body, whether to prevent or induce a major or a minor condition; as someone said, "There are no incurable conditions, but there are sometimes incurable people."

The following is a dramatic example of how even an advanced case of cancer can be reversed through understanding of the subconscious.

Mrs. M., a 40-year-old married woman and mother of five children, was referred to me by a family friend — a physician. Mrs. M. suffered from cancer of the stomach which had spread to her lungs and lymph nodes. She was vomiting blood and had lost a great deal of weight; she was pale and emaciated. Her illness was declared terminal by examining doctors, and she had been given only two months to live. The chemotherapy treatment no longer seemed to help.

Her marriage had suffered a number of problems; she said that she only lived with her husband out of a sense of duty. Her illness had started several months prior to my first seeing her and had progressed quite rapidly. It appeared that the onset of the cancer was marked by an argument with her husband, which led to a decision to divorce him. She also experienced nightmares in which she killed him. Obviously, her intentions toward him were something less than honorable.

To maintain confidentiality, I saw her at my house, instructing her in guided imagery. I taught her to communicate with her subconscious.. Her subconscious shouted that it wanted to kill her, just as she had killed someone else — a man. Naturally, the reply to her subconscious was that she had never even attempted to kill a man. It had only "happened" in a nightmare. Sibil (this was the name of her subconscious) insisted that she had killed a man; not in the dream, but in reality. After that, Mrs. M. willfully refused to discuss this any further. Nevertheless, I continued to urge Mrs. M. to persuade Sibil to give her "a grace period" in order to more thoroughly understand why she killed a man. She told Sibil she would then pay for the murder according to the universal law of *karma*, or cause and effect. Sibil was also told by Mrs. M. that if she did indeed commit a murder, she is ready to pay the debt for it. Sibil agreed, and therefore increased her red blood count and stopped her vomiting, in order that Mrs. M.could learn more about the problem. As one can see, the conscious mind, with its superior reasoning, can rule the subconscious. It is a matter of time, persistence, and a kindly but firm dictation to the subconscious of what you think is right. Indeed, Sibil increased gradually the red blood count and almost stopped Mrs. M. from vomiting for the following two weeks.

At the end of the period, she again began to deteriorate and vomited a great deal of blood. Her red blood count dropped to a point where her oncologist considered it necessary to hospitalize her again for a blood transfusion and inpatient care. However, before she was hospitalized, I convinced Mrs. M. to let me regress her into a previous life where we just might find the answer to her problem, though she said she did not believe in reincarnation. She eventually agreed, as she felt she had nothing to lose.

Through hypnosis, Mrs. M. learned she lived in London in 1905. She was 17 years old at the time and a beautiful girl. Her name was Sibil, like the name of her subconscious, and she worked as a servant in a rich man's house. Her master, a widower, was old, ugly, and fat, but he was kind to her and gave her a number of valuable presents. Finally, she started living with hen as his mistress. However, she discovered him to be possessive, and he barred her from going out alone. Despite these restrictions, she occasionally had amorous affairs with younger men.

Learning about this, the old man confined her to the house. She found this intolerable. As a result, she reached a fateful decision. One day she procured an amount of concentrated sulfuric acid and poured it in his meal. He began to vomit blood and suffered a great deal. She ran from the house. In a short time she moved with one of her boyfriends to the country, some distance from London.

Another servant later told her that her protector died before the doctor could do anything for him. Sibil died at the age of 28 of a digestive infection.

Under hypnosis it was also learned that the man she killed in that earlier life was her present husband.

Mrs. M. was brought out of hypnosis and we discussed her problems. She was instructed to talk with Sibil and explain to her that she had accepted the gravity of her crime and knew she must pay for it. But she should not pay for it with her life, for then she would not be able to help people in her present employment as a social worker. Only if she is alive and healthy, could she dedicate herself. She told Sibil that she would also do volunteer work in her church and be good to her children. Divorce was no longer to be an issue in her life. The important thing is that she is going to pay her karmic debt. The result was that Sibil promised to make her well. Mrs. M. was instructed to continue to talk with Sibil on a daily basis, reinforcing that agreement, and becoming the best of friends.

Mrs. M.'s clinical condition and laboratory findings continued to show gradual improvement. To the astonishment of her oncologist, the cancer went into complete remission in two months. Even the spread of the cancer to her lungs had cleared.

Recently I had the opportunity to talk with Mrs. M., who reported everything was fine. Though she divorced her husband, she is dedicated to her work and her children.

The example of Mrs. M.'s advanced cancer and its cure supports the value of unlocking a conflict in the past, even in a previous life, and communicating with the subconscious to bring about health, even in an apparently terminal situation. However, I must stress that orthodox medical and surgical procedures should always be considered in conjunction with such unorthodox methods. In this case, orthodox therapy failed where unorthodox treatment succeeded.

In the subconscious, the memory bank, again like that of a computer, has stored in it, in well-identifiable shelves, picture word clusters of memories from this lifetime and previous ones. That may explain why Mrs. M. could bring her memories from her past life as Sibil — though her body and brain had died — because her subconscious continued to carry the memory bank into this lifetime with her new body and brain. Under certain conditions which permit better attunement into the subconscious (such as hypnosis, self-hypnosis, guided imagery methods, dreams, etc.) the memory bank can be tapped and important memories, sometimes in the form of dream-like images, can be revealed. These memories are often accompanied by other corresponding sensations, impressions, and emotions which clarify the problems a person currently experiences. Through the conscious awareness of the problem, it may dissolve in some half of the cases, though another half may need additional conscious repetition programming through different methods.

By analogy, psychoanalysis, through repetitious expression of intellectual (conscious) insight into the problems, in time brings about emotional (subconscious) insight. The shortcomings here are the vagueness and the extended time needed to accomplish the goal or treatment and the fact that the goal may never be reached because past life conflicts remain untouched.

The subconscious is the source of emotions and desires such as anger, fear, anxiety, etc. One may ask, "What about love? Isn't love an emotion?: No, it Is not! What we refer to as personal love for a spouse, a parent, a child, a brother, a sister, a dear friend, is merely emotional attachment. Real love is Divine Love, which the animal is not capable of experiencing. Divine Love — is an attribute of the Union Soul-G-d only. Divine Love or Christ Love is unconditional: I love you no matter whether you love me, no matter who you are. I expect nothing in exchange, even if you hate me, I love you. This is Christ Love.

161

Jesus demonstrated this love when he forgave his executioners, knowing they did not know what they were doing. They were blinded by their subconscious.

Though the animal is capable of emotional attachment, it is still the most advanced and positive expression it can give. The emotional attachment is a conditional "love": "I love if you love me." "I will be nice to you if you are nice to me." This so-called "love" of the subconscious is like a roller-coaster that goes up and down. One cannot rely on It. It is like a friendship between two young children. One moment they are the best of friends, playing happily with each other; the next moment they are in a fight, then a moment later they make up again, and so on and so on. It' one attends a divorce court for only one day, one can see how people who presumably once loved each other are at one another's throats. Is this love? Real love is possible only when it is unconditional, and it can come only from the conscious and superconscious. If people who love each other will be more conscious, they must truly create the right conditions to love one another.

We live in a world of addictions. People become addicted at the level of their emotions and desires. What is an addiction? Rosita Rodriguez gave us a very good definition'. "It is an emotional attachment that is exaggerated." Though it hurts you, the subconscious still cannot let go of it. Though people are addicted to cigarettes, alcohol, drugs, food, a spouse, television, work, it is only the conscious mind that may stop such an addiction. But not only by being aware of it, but by consciously reprogramming the subconscious for as long as it is necessary to overcome the addiction.

I learned (from Rosita Rodriguez) of a method to effectively heal such addictions. It is called the Shouting Affirmation. It works very much like that employed by evangelists who perform a "miracle" by having a paralyzed person in a wheelchair shout, "I am healed!" repeatedly from the top of his lungs, and start him walking after 15 to 20 years of complete paralysis. This is not a miracle, but simply. the subconscious finally responding by agreeing to the conscious mind's shouting. It is like a big brother starting to play basketball and the little brother begging, "Me too! Me too!" During the shouting affirmation, the subconscious does not literally say,

"Me too!" Rather it builds up a powerful emotional response which may be an immense flood of joy, laughter, crying, or a mixture. Since the subconscious is the source of our emotions, this means it has finally agreed with the shouting affirmation. An example of shouting affirmation that works even with heroin addicts, even after five years or so of failure, (about 65 % of them in methadone clinics, supported addicts by millions of dollars of taxpayers' money) is as follows: "I stopped heroin!" This affirmation is shouted to himself by the addict, loudly and repeatedly, until a strong emotional response from the subconscious is manifested. It may take from five to fifteen minutes to obtain this kind of response; but once it is manifested, an agreement between the conscious and the subconscious takes place, and usually no further repetition of the exercise is necessary. Moreover, there are no withdrawal symptoms because the subconscious is programmed to control the physical body; it is now cooperative for the first time; therefore no "temper tantrums" or withdrawal symptoms are necessary.

Using this same principle, one may rid oneself of smoking, alcohol abuse, and other addictions. Most persons don't particularly care to shout, but there is no reason one cannot choose the basement or a lonely spot in the forest to carry it out.

I recall a patient of mine, a 36-year-old married woman from Tennessee. Mrs. G. came to my office for hypnosis in order to quit smoking. She was smoking about three and ,one half packs of cigarettes a day. I explained to her the shouting affirmation method, and I told her she can succeed by this way alone — saving her several hypnosis fees. She left my office saying she would do it. After about four weeks she telephoned to thank me, that since she had begun the shouting affirmation, she not only had not smoked a single cigarette (with no withdrawal symptoms) but her hand automatically retracted from a cigarette pack if she reached for it!

Another attribute of the conscious mind is the psyche or intuition. Here I must stress that this is not to be confused with the superior, or spiritual, intuition of the superconscious. As mentioned before, this ability of the subconscious has to do with extrasensory perception, precognition, psychokinesis, and so forth. This is our "gut feeling" or "sixth sense." From previous lives perhaps the subconscious remembers how witches were burned at the stake for displaying this ability. Here and there we find ourselves successfully using this "sense" in business and other areas of activity. Sometimes we think the telephone will ring and somebody we want to talk with will be at the other end of the line. It happens exactly so. At other times, we wake up in the morning a fraction of a second prior to the alarm.

Psychic development of the subconscious takes place as the person develops spiritually. Forcing the subconscious to exhibit extraordinary abilities before there is sufficient conscious awareness and spiritual development may create confusion and a detachment from reality. A psychotic breakdown may ensue. That is why emphasis should be placed on spiritual development, on our becoming consciously aware. Then the psychic abilities of the subconscious will fall into place as well. It is easier and safer to develop these abilities hand in hand with spiritual growth. Therefore, it is a good idea to deprogram the subconscious from any misconceptions of the past regarding these abilities, and eventually reprogram it to positively and successfully utilize these gifts. A great deal of psychic healing is accomplished through such subconscious attributes.

Another characteristic of the subconscious is that it forms conditioned reflexes, automatic skills and habits. This includes our biases, prejudices, false beliefs, false principles, false pride, etc. We are programmed in our subconscious from womb to tomb, so to speak. And then, if you will, from womb to tomb and from tomb to womb, through many lifetimes. Through gravitational pull, the planets are the first to put their imprint on our subconscious at the time of birth. We know how the full moon creates tidal changes through its magnetic pull. By the same mechanism, our subconscious is influenced by a certain configuration of planets at our birth. This first influence at the beginning of a life has a domino effect, since any later influence will tend to take the same direction; however, the personality initiated in this way is a product of the subconscious; it is the subconscious personality. The conscious and the superconscious play no part in it. As a matter of fact, the union of conscious and superconscious, which is G-d, cannot be influenced by the planets, or the stars, since G-d created them!

On the contrary, it makes sense that G-d can influence them. That is why through will power from the conscious one can undo any negative trait that was cast on the subconscious by the planets. But again, because most people are unconscious most of the time, it makes sense to pay attention to the astrological personality characteristics of an individual born on such and such a date, as this is another exercise into becoming conscious of one's subconscious, therefore understanding better its assets and liabilities and mastering them constructively.

CHAPTER EIGHTEEN
Astrology and Spiritual Growth

Hippocrates, the father of medicine, said nearly 2,400 years ago: "A physician without a knowledge of astrology has no right to call himself a physician." Astrology, the oldest known science of our culture, dates back some 5,000 years. It certainly would have disappeared long ago if it did not have some validity. Medicine, concentrating on the trees, lost sight of the forest. One application of astrology has been to establish with mathematical precision where we come from and where we are going in our life experience. In other words, astrology instructs us (in accordance with the position of the moon at the time of our birth) in what astrological sign will mathematically characterize our past lives' experiences. Also, astrology can tell us that what we need to learn in this lifetime is precisely opposite to what we didn't learn earlier. All this is done to balance us karmically.

What is truly amazing is that the mathematical chart which indicates the calculated positions of the moon during different years confirms the authenticity of a majority of my past life research cases. Under hypnosis, the subjects gave me dates of birth in previous lives which were very much the expected, logical continuity of life experience in this lifetime, where the birthdate is different. The research volunteers knew nothing about such a mathematical chart; yet under hypnosis they gave the date of birth in a previous life which strongly indicates — in nice mathematical terms — the necessity for acquiring in this lifetime experiences which have not been acquired in previous lives.

For purposes of this present discussion, let us review the case of Mary F., mentioned earlier. Mary gave me her present birthdate as July 22, 1972 and her previous life's birthdate as February 2, 1862. Though these dates would fall under different signs of the twelve sun signs of the astrological zodiac, Leo and Aquarius, respectively, in the chart with the calculated moon position in the northern hemisphere of the earth at the time of birth, these dates will both fall under the sign of

Capricorn. This means that this little girl failed to completely learn her Capricorn lesson in the previous life. Therefore, she must continue the same experience in this lifetime. It means that the average of possibly thousands of past lives will fall under the sign of Cancer, which is 180 degrees opposite her Capricorn. Her Leo sun sign now is merely a static one that indicates the personality of her subconscious, which will undertake to accomplish the lesson of Capricorn. The subconscious is endowed, as we said, with psychic ability, a sort of magnetic pen which will orient it to be reborn for the life experience which is missing, according to the karmic balance. And, as most important decisions here and in between physical lives are made by the subconscious, it is no wonder it happens this way.

People imagine that after leaving this plane they become wiser! Not so, as people are as unconscious in the astral plane as they are here. Wisdom is earned through experience. Hence, it is imperative *now* to become conscious in order to stop this spinning wheel of karma, and to rejoin the Creator forever.

In any case, this is another way of becoming conscious of astrological influences upon the subconscious, whether they have to do with the static personality of the subconscious in this lifetime, or with the purpose of life experiences the subconscious acquires throughout many lives.

In the case of Mary F., her subconscious has to learn to overcome the negatives of the sign of Cancer (softness, excess of emotionality, sickness, dependency) and learn the positive aspects of Capricorn (firmness, maturity, health, and independence.) The Leo sun sign in this lifetime is a powerful one that can assist Mary to accomplish her subconscious mission.

What thrilled me most is that the above-mentioned chart of the moon's nodes' positions confirmed my research work into past life and reincarnation in a majority of cases as a viable hypothesis, while my research work confirmed the authenticity of that chart. This in itself simplified a great deal of research.

Continuing the programming of the subconscious, there appear other authority figures in our lives who play conscious roles for us, as if we do not have our own conscious mind. Psychoanalysts put a great deal of emphasis on the relationship between mother and infant. This is obviously true, for it creates another domino effect in the way the mother programs the infant's subconscious. But a great portion of whom we are when born, unfortunately, may not be taken into account by psychoanalysts, as they don't deal with past lives.

Next, our parents tell us what is right and what is wrong, because they have been programmed in their subconscious believes they are right. Often they are wrong, as they too were programmed in their subconsciousness by their parents, and in their training. The army tells us when to die, and when not to die, and we are forbidden to consciously question or refuse to go to war.

Religion may play soul and G-d by telling us that we either go to hell or not. We "hit bottom" when we allow the subconscious to run our lives. I am neither for nor against any religion, but I think religions would help people more if they would stop playing G-d for them; rather, they should make people aware that each has the Soul-G-d within oneself, as Jesus meant it originally. As a matter of fact, the major religions all derive from the understanding of the three levels of consciousness, only that religious leaders were subconscious too. Perhaps with more conscious awareness, many of them used their positions of responsibility to exercise power and gain money, for this purpose they had to play directly on the people's subconscious. This is what still happens with many religious cults.

Hopefully, many religions are now becoming more liberal, which may encourage greater conscious responsibility on the part of each individual. After all, as mentioned in Matthew in the New Testament, correct praying is done on the Mount (G-d) and "in the closet of one's Soul." This is the prayer that reaches G-d. Praying only to make an impression on others, or being impressed by the building and the decorations of the place of worship, is only for the subconscious. That is why most prayers remain unanswered, because they are addressed to the subconscious rather than to G-d. Many a time we made a G-d out of the animal, and the animal feels all powerful, and we let it destroy our lives. Obviously, it does not know now to make prayers come true, or it wants to flex its muscle, indicating a rejection of prayer. Effective prayer appears to be helping (consciously) oneself positively. In this way G-d helps too. (As G-d and soul are one unit, and are made up of the same image). Begging the subconscious — the third person — may end up in failure. In effective prayer, one makes the subconscious do positive things inspired by G-d's goodness and relaxation, like Sabbath's rest. This is a must in order to make such a process successful.

The media programs our subconscious, telling us what to eat, what to drink. People, especially children in this country, are "glued" to the television for an average of six hours a day. In the medical school the subconscious is programmed, too, and many times based on false assumptions. This is true with any profession or occupation.

After all this horrendous programming of my subconscious at a party or other social gathering, I may very solemnly give "my opinion" in such and such a matter. Nonsense! It is not my opinion. It would be my opinion only if I consciously tested it and it worked.

CHAPTER NINETEEN
Subconscious Development

The key to development is becoming conscious. But becoming conscious doesn't mean always becoming spiritual. It depends on whether the conscious growth is used for material pursuit of the subconscious or spiritual development. The first is called Anti-Christ, while the last is called Christ. The Christ movement is, in my view, where the light will come from. But, since this book is addressed to the reader's conscious mind and not the subconscious, I would leave it up to you, reader, to decide after the proper testing. And if it works for you, you will *know* I am right.

Finally, the last attribute of the subconscious I want to stress is its limited reasoning, varying in our society from two to five and one half years of age, with an average of three-and-a-quarter years of age.

A concept of paramount importance is the ego, the bridge between the conscious and subconscious mind, and many times confused with the negative attributes of the subconscious. In reality the "animal" (subconscious) does not kill for the sake of killing, but only when hungry, only when its territory has been intruded upon. Murder, pride, envy, jealousy, intrigue are some of ego's negative characteristics. The ego represents the subconscious which has borrowed some of the conscious attributes and is boasting how great it is. The more consciously aware and spiritual a person becomes, the more he understands the subconscious and the less manifest are the negative ego attributes.

The following chart presents a general overview of subconscious development. In order to adequately understand and help an individual, the age of his or her subconscious must be known. More precise determinations can be obtained through detailed psychological questionnaires and corresponding scales.

SUBCONSCIOUS DEVELOPMENT

AGE LEVELS	CHARACTERISTICS	DEPENDENCY DEGREE	SELF-AWARENESS*
1	Instinctive, sensual, sexual: body consciousness	Entirely dependent	Almost nonexistent
2	Affectionate, emotional, evolving personality or character	Very dependent	Very limited self-awareness
3	Elementary skills; elementary social awareness and interaction	Dependent	At times self-awareness
4	Advanced and creative skills; few social skills and self-consciousness	At times dependent	Within a 50-50 range of self-awareness
5	Elementary ethics; limited responsibility for oneself, some regard for others; more advanced social skills	Often independent	Raised self-awareness
6	Responsibility for oneself, regard and a certain degree of responsibility for other people; now it can survive through its own abilities	Mostly independent	Highly raised self-awareness
7	Leadership, initiative; superior skill, creativity. High degree of survival skills, uses past memories coupled with intellect in solving problems. Extremely cooperative.	Entirely independent	Entirely self-aware

*Usually parallels conscious awareness

The foregoing chart presents a general set of characteristics a child displays from one to seven years old. To some extent it parallels the levels of character organization in the psychoanalytic interpretation. In this view, aggression is emphasized as our main instinct, well at work into the second year of life. Generally, starting with the third year, the sexual instinct begins to manifest, culminating at five to seven (subconscious) years of age, with high morals and appropriate channeling or sublimation of the sexual drive. As most people are operating at the level of their subconscious most of the time, it makes sense to identify the child's developmental age levels with this development.

According to this chart, derived from various milestones in the child's development, at age one the subconscious is projecting the following characteristics: instinctive, sensual, sexual, and body consciousness. Its degree of dependency is considered complete. The self-awareness which parallels conscious awareness is almost nonexistent. People with such a young subconscious in our society are usually found to be severely mentally ill or chronically confined to mental wards. This is not to indicate that a regular person does not express himself at this level or at any other of the seven age levels at certain times. But such a person's subconscious developmental level will be found at a level on which the individual expresses himself most of the times.

At age two the subconscious is predominately affectionate and emotional. The personality starts to unfold. The subconscious is dependent and there is little conscious awareness.

At age three elementary skills and basic social awareness begin to develop. The subconscious is, however, still dependent upon others. Occasionally, at this level, the subconscious exhibits self-awareness.

Some anthropological studies indicate that man dates back as early as three-and-one-half million years. It apparently took that long for homo sapiens to reach the age level of three years of the subconscious, through thousands of reincarnations. At this point the speed of growth of the subconscious is phenomenal; within two or three generations in suitable consciousness-raising circumstances, the subconscious may

173

even reach seven the highest in its development, the age of reasoning.

Like a child between the ages of three and four years old, the subconscious becomes "a little pest," constantly asking questions, no longer accepting old beliefs, struggling to be less dependent. The child is gaining control of himself and his environment. That is why in our society, which has a subconscious of about three-and-a-quarter, there is such a raise in consciousness and great turmoil as a consequence. But between three and five years of age of the subconscious exists a transition period, in which there is a shifting back and forth from being subconscious to being conscious and vice versa, resulting in confusion. This confusion gradually intensifies, bringing in great part discontent, stress, unhappiness, illness, and destructive interpersonal relationships.

As shown in the chart, there is now partial self or conscious awareness, and the person sees "the pen" as a pen while conscious, and as "an orange" while subconscious. However, the peak of confusion occurs between the ages of three-and-one-half and four-and-one-half, where unfortunately, most of our leaders are to be found, including those in the professions. This is why people complain of a crisis in leadership. This is why youth is faced with a so-called identity crisis. This is why the rate of divorce is increasing drastically. During this stage of subconscious development, unlike before age three, when people were more or less at the same level, people develop at different rates now and like children, after three years of age, their speed of growth is extremely rapid and widely differs from one child to another. This explains why people may not get along with each other any longer. For instance, spouses that were at the same age level before, after several years of living together, may find themselves in different worlds, like strangers who cannot understand each other any longer. One perhaps grows faster than the other, or apart, due to different pursuits.

Conscious awakening obviously boosts subconscious growth, because the more consciously related or spiritual one becomes the more the subconscious assimilates and grows into maturity. If there is a difference of more than four to six months between the two subconsciouses of spouses, for instance, they will not be able to get along easily with each other. If the gap is wider, let us say a year, they may even get into a serious fight. Take as an example two normal children — a three-year-old and a four-year-old who play together. Naturally, the four-year-old will want to be the boss and the three-year-old will start screaming. As a result, the four-year-old will assert his sovereignty, and the three-year-old will scream all the louder. In such a relationship no one can be happy.

Much the same thing happens with grown-ups, since 90 percent of them are relating to one another 90 percent of the time at the age level of their subconscious. This explains why chronological age does not play an important role. Most important in any interpersonal relationships are the ages of the subconscious. Thus the so-called "generation gap" has to do with the difference in the subconscious age between parents and children. Conceivably a child could have an older subconscious than his parents do, though it may be the other way around. In this light we can state that leadership in this society must be determined by correct appraisal and periodic reappraisal of subconscious age levels, in order to fit that individual in the proper position. Imagine a foreman with a two-and-one-half-year-old subconscious, bossing around a worker with a three-and-one-half-year-old subconscious! It is not going to work. The same thing applies to education. In educating children and adults, the right methods should primarily take into account the individual's subconscious age level.

At age five of the subconscious, the turmoil of confusion stops, as people for the first time see "the pen" as a pen, all the time. While they saw it as "an orange" and believed it, they were under three years old, and were happy, for they did not question a lot of things. They were "happy" in ignorance. The real happiness they start testing, now, when they know it. At this age spouses realize they do not own each other. They respect each other's needs, and if they follow the same soul-growth path they can live together in amity. The only reason warranting the ending of such a relationship is if it hinders conscious awakening and spiritual growth. If such individuals decide that their relationship does not work, they can easily terminate it, since they are often independent. Now they no longer depend on one another's subconscious, though their subconscious depends on their own conscious mind. Here we find heightened self-awareness going hand-in-hand with increased conscious awareness. At this age basic ethics are common, as well as a responsibility for self, concern for others, and advanced social skills.

A subconscious six-year-old is rather rare. It is responsible for self, shows concern and some responsibility for others, and is able to survive on its own. This mature subconscious is independent and self-aware. The conscious mind in this case is obviously very much in charge.

It was found that children in under-developed counties, orphaned by war, could not survive on their own after the war if under six years of age; helpless, they would starve to death if not found in time. On the other hand, children over six years old, would knock on doors, seek food and shelter, and eventually save themselves. Likewise the six-year-old subconscious can survive on its own. To illustrate, let us take a hypothetical example of a multiple car accident in which the conscious minds of the drivers have become retarded from heavy drinking. Those drivers involved who have a subconscious six years or older will pull out of the accident without major injuries, most likely, while those under six will be badly injured or even killed. Such an example is quite remote from reality because a person with a six-year-old subconscious would not get drunk in the first place! But as most people are unconscious most of the time, without necessarily being intoxicated, this example applies in any case.

A seven-year-old subconscious is an extreme rarity. At this age, the subconscious excels in leadership, initiative, creativity, resourcefulness, uses past memories and the intellect to solve problems, and is extremely cooperative. It is completely independent and self-aware. A so-called "resurrection" takes place within the individual, with the conscious mind separating from the subconscious, each living an independent existence.

Such resurrection can be reached through special exercises of conscious awakening, when the subconscious is more than three years old. What is interesting is that at seven years of age, the subconscious does not have to be caught by the conscious, like the three-year-old child playing with matches, but this time the seven year old comes by itself to the conscious to ask for advice. Moreover, it delves into past memories, including those of past lives, in order to solve problems, and not repeat past mistakes.

The linkage between different age levels of the subconscious and health care is of paramount importance. When we are speaking of a new age in health care, we are really speaking of a very ancient belief that science and philosophy must work together. Illness of the body is recognized as a very real occurrence in need of correction, or better yet, prevention. Also, we must recognize a special presence of a consciousness in the body, in fact, in every cell of the body.

As one advances through the levels of consciousness, one comes to know that every animal body, be it ours or that of another, is governed by consciousness. It is that consciousness that we have been ignoring in traditional health care.

Because this consciousness cannot be measured in all its forms and can therefore not be duplicated by science, it is often rejected by the medical profession or put into a category of fantasy. Even when healing through consciousness is proved effective, many prominent physicians refuse to grant it credence. And yet, from my own experience, I know that patients have been healed through the use of consciousness. I know of some physicians who applied guided imagery techniques in treating their patients, in dealing with certain types of pain, but eventually abandoned such techniques because they found it too "unsafe."

Modern medicine knows that people can make themselves sick, that certain diseases are manifested as stress symptoms, for instance; that the patient without the will to live cannot be made to live. Years ago many doctors knew that certain types of ulcers, hypertension, angina, and various other problems were related to emotional stress, but they were still not ready to accept that all dysfunctions were operating on an emotional or consciousness level. My own clinical experience, however, has shown quite the reverse. This is supported by the many, many cases that I have been able to investigate. I now am certain that all illnesses have initial emotional causes, as part of our subconscious activity. We are all subject to such activity because we are emotional creatures, and as such are subject to such changes as long as we live in the body.

Medicine has called this phenomenon "psychosomatic," which has an unhappy connotation for a patient who might think this means he is imagining the illness. Nothing could be further from the truth. The experience of illness is the same. It is true that illness is an illusion, but it is experienced just the same. It makes us aware of crying for help. Sometimes the subconscious says, "I have an existence here, a good animal existence, that I could live. You are not letting me live it. I am getting out, out of the body." The animal in us does not reason well. It might begin to think it can live more happily in another body. If we do not give it an opportunity to live happily, it may find a way to do so.

Medicine has often decried claims of a healing because the condition was seen as only psychosomatic. Well, so is the cure. There is no such thing as something being psychosomatic. Of course, there are psychological reasons for being sick, but that does not mean that the patient is not sick, that the patient is not suffering, and that whatever we are doing, whether it is healing or medical ministration, is not effective. In many cases, if the subconscious is not reached, a cure cannot take place.

When we consider that since the subconscious brought on the condition, the subconscious must remove it, the whole process of getting sick and getting well is soon recognized as a psychosomatic one. And that is what it Is.

The study of a person's emotional life can tell us what is wrong with his or her body; conversely, it is possible to tell what emotional problems caused the illness. No definite categorization can be made yet, but the major illnesses, the big killers (for which traditional medicine can do little) show that going to the source of the problem is the secret of healing. In other words, through consciousness, it is possible to know the origins of most major illnesses and research the reasons for the lesser known physical problems. Through conscious awareness one can specifically understand social and economic pressures that influence our health as well as the structure of the personality and relationships with one another. Relationships are at the bottom of many of our problems.

CHAPTER TWENTY
The Subconscious and Illness

Through clinical experience and research — much of it corroborated by Rosita Rodriguez — I found that certain subconscious age levels are more prone to certain physical problems. The physical age of the patient is an additional factor. We find variation in both the number and intensity of illnesses in other countries and in other races — those which have different subconscious age levels — than our North American society. In several primitive societies, for instance, there is a nearly total absence of cancer. They simply do not possess the emotional character to produce cancer. In most of these societies arthritis is also unknown. They are not at the point yet where they think they must always be "right." They have not yet reached the three-year-old level of the subconscious. As these societies grow in consciousness, a few months at a time, we will find them becoming subject to entirely different types of illnesses.

Some of those illnesses that afflicted civilized society years ago, and that we still find in primitive societies, have all but disappeared. Certainly we can thank modern medicine for this. Some of these diseases do not occur in our society any more because we no longer live under those conditions. By the same token, younger societies are not yet reacting to the stress conditions we have in our own lives, so they have not inherited these particular problems yet.

Anthropologists Gregory Bateson and Margaret Mead did extensive research with people all over the world. They found out that if strangers entered their "comfort zone" with new teachings and attempted to impose a new social structure or a new religious belief on them, they inevitably suffered illness. Their subconscious simply could not cope with such an intervention; they were hindered, as it were, from progressing through their states of evolution. We now know that missionaries did untold damage to many cultures by rudely imposing their moral values and religious beliefs on susceptible natives. The result was much human suffering.

Scientists have long tried to explain away certain illnesses as being brought from one country to the next by sailors or other agents. This is not necessarily true. Rather, it was the 'level of the subconscious that was not properly age addressed. These people would have evolved in their own way, probably in a very healthy way, if such intervention had not occurred. That was the real crime of the missionaries.

Can we see what is happening to the health of the world? If we know that the health of an individual and of the nation depends on subconscious age levels, then we must have materia medica of a different order. If we stay within this law and work within it, we will accomplish something for ourselves and others. If we do not, we will continue to foster ignorance; and people will continue to remain sick rather than get well.

This much, then, we know: illness can be predicted, diagnosed, treated, and prevented according to the age levels of the subconscious. This means that for physicians and other health professionals, the subconscious age level of a person is vitally important in determining first, why the patient is ill and second, what kind of treatment is indicated. As mentioned earlier, a healer usually works with one method. It may be the laying on of hands, prayer, manipulation, or healing with the assistance of spirit guides, or psychic surgery. Each of these methods is usually suited to the specific subconscious age level of that society in which we find the healer. Younger or older societies are not taken into consideration, or younger or older subconscious age levels that fall out of the norm in their society. This is important.

Rosita Rodriguez used to express amazement that people came so far to the Philippines for healing — that is, to a younger society than their own. She saw that psychic surgery was attracting people who were younger in their subconscious. They were not really satisfied with the level of' healing in their own country, could not identify with the level of healing they were receiving. Of course, healers are usually not aware that their method is suitable only to their society, and they use it on all people; however, only the age level addressed (those who fall within at least one year of the acceptable healing method) will be helped.

It is interesting to note that as a general rule, the correct age level is attracted to the right healer. They seem to feel that this is where they are going to receive help. In medicine, both patients and physician are so programmed in their subconscious that they both believe orthodox medicine to be the only answer. We have been programmed to believe that authority, particularly the authority coming from those who are our elders in knowledge, our teachers, or even the printed page — is absolute. Such figures may know much in their specific field, but we must consider that they do not know everything. No one does. We must be cautious, for instance, in recommending books for others. This should be done only after knowing the person, and knowing whether they are consciously aware and discriminating. One can never be too careful. I recall that in earlier years my colleagues and I would study medical texts and at times think we had the disease or the syndrome we were studying. Some of my colleagues actually got sick from such study! We need to become much more conscious about how to receive certain information and how to dispose of it. This is particularly true of the physician who, unlike the healer, may not have the choice of treating those he chooses.

The early country doctor had an advantage over the modern physician in that he worked with people individually. Even though he may not have known the laws in the way I am describing them, he knew that different personalities required different treatment. Today, the physician is so busy he does not have the time to treat patients with enough attention to individual differences.

There is a difference in health care and how we can care for ourselves and people's health. Careful judgment should be used; you must know yourself and your age level. As a physician or health professional, you must know your patient's age level if you want to be accurate. Then the percentage of cures will increase. We may regress to a lower age level or progress to a higher one under certain conditions, but our subconscious age level is where we generally function most of the time. For instance, at the subconscious age level up to, let us say, approximately one year and a half, life is a total survival struggle. This is the time for infectious diseases, when we are ignorant and dependent, when we are total believers. From two to two-and-a-half years old of the subconscious the person

181

is young emotionally; he is often sick; he needs much repetition and direction and cannot understand spiritual concepts, though he can be motivated to kindness and good for human reasons; he needs motivation in basic skills. These are simple people, peaceful and happy in a healthy routine setting. They have a tribal dependency. They may work in industry as rank and file employees. Their education is limited.

Up to the subconscious age level of two-and-a-half years, which we know to be the emotional level, we have had to deal with the serious emotional illnesses, the virus-connected problems; cancer is one of them. Some people believe they have to suffer. This derives out of our belief systems and is incorporated in expressions of guilt and martyrdom; until we make ourselves ill.

Up to the age of two-and-a-half, a person trusts and believes the healer or physician completely. He is to be treated through belief. They will get well if they are prayed over, or given a placebo. They will get well in any event if ,they trust you and believe in you, because their subconscious says: "Oh, I am going to have to give that up because he is going to straighten all these things out." They are not old enough subconsciously yet to figure out for themselves that the conditions are not going to be straightened out. They allow themselves to be healed, in many instances. At least for a time, by the physician or healer simply because they think everything is going to go away. Just as with little children, when they cry, you pick them up and you "make it all well." There is something to be said about this making it all well. Their hurt feelings and their hurt knee, and the whole problem is made all well because they are still on this level of trusting and believing.

From here on out, we have to proceed a bit slower because the next half year, between two-and-a-half and three years, is a strong, guilt-laden time. Such emotions are producing most of the problems. We are just becoming aware of ourselves, and everyone is telling us how bad or how wrong we are. Though we are trying hard, nothing is coming out right. This is often the time for heart and vascular problems. The subconscious is not capable of taking responsibility for itself yet. It is reaching in that area from time to time, but it is still at the point: "Well it happened to me, a heart problem, because my father had it." If they are really smart they say: "You made me sick because you did so and so . . ." They are not able to take responsibility for themselves yet. They are easily influenced in their opinions by outside opinions about conditions and treatments and they often get sick again after a cure. Much of this is particularly relevant in the case of psychic surgery, because the majority of patients who undergo it are between the age levels of two-and-a-half and three years old. And in many instances, they are having to face going home and proving their cures and their trip and why they went to this 66 quack" to be cured in the first place. Some of them are so worried about this that healing is prevented. They may fear: "Oh, my G-d, this (illness) had better be gone by the time I get home, or what are they going to say? Nobody is going to believe me." This produces anxiety. They should be concerning themselves about themselves. They are not old enough yet on the subconscious age level to know this. Also, they want the rest of the world to know about this. They want to share this and they want to be right about it. And of course, as you know, we cannot be right about these kinds of things.

Now what often happens in many of these instances is that some of these people come home with a healing certified and visible. They are walking now when they had not been walking before. And, their doctor says he cannot find this on the blood test any more. And after the relatives got through with them, they got sick again, because they are easily influenced by others. Somebody shows them a paper and says, "Two years ago this was written up, this guy is a quack, didn't you see it? Well, even though you were healed, there is no way he could have healed you, right?" It turns the whole thing around again. This happens over and over.

The evangelist-healer Katherine Kuhlman encountered such patients. The patients would get well on the stage and two days later they would be in a wheelchair again. If the patient walks two steps, his organic nervous system is no longer damaged. That patient can be brought back with physical therapy and the proper care to a normal life. But if I his mind says no, if his subconscious says he has to be sick, the doctor will tell him: "You will never walk again, you cannot," it follows that he will not. So it is at that age that we are very easily

183

influenced. We are still believers, although not as completely as a two or two-and-a-half-year-old would be.

This is also the time when we go in for scientific methods. We are looking for higher education during that age level already, and we believe that scientists really know something; so we want to be treated in scientific ways, but by belief. These are not the patients who cooperate with their doctors. They 'just like to lie down and say: "Do something!" And if it does not work because of their own emotional condition, then they feel the doctor was not any good. If they go to a healer and his treatment does not work, then the healer is seen as a quack.

At this age, orthodox religiosity and righteousness are prevalent; there are established work ethics and people are intellectually motivated. More refined emotions are displayed, though strongly expressed. Illnesses at this age become more sophisticated. They are more stable economically and materially, ambitious, charitable, dependent on marriage, relatives and friends. These people may work in industry and they have at least a high school education, and often higher. They are usually line and office supervisors, and in the lower and middle management. Involvement in small business, the trades or a young pioneering profession is common to this age group.

The next age level, from three to three-and-a-half years, creates problems mostly brought on by stress. These are the people who are already in a fast-moving society. This does not mean that they are living in a different society than ourselves, but they have more pressure-filled jobs. They receive more social pressure, for instance, and through this stress, of course, they manifest all the stress symptoms. These are the people with the hypertension, ulcers, cancers and heart problems. Think of all the problems that stress causes! Though some might respond to someone saying: "You know, you should try Transcendental Meditation. That will help bring down your blood pressure," they are skeptical. Such people are orthodox because they are educated. Between the age levels of three and three-and-a-half they have made sure they got an education. Now they know something. They know what one has to go through to graduate with a degree. They figure doubly that what one gets with the degree is absolute knowledge; but they do not always recognize that this is not necessarily so, that there is other knowledge in the universe that they are not aware of yet. So they are very orthodox; they are skeptical. In the long run, they are easier to work with than the two-and-a-half or three-year-old, because if you take time you can logically present your position to them. You can help them through a good, logical presentation. Some in this category can be taught to stay well.

Individuals with a subconscious age level from about three-and-a-half to four present consciousness conflicts as their major source of illness. We have quite a separation of the subconscious and the conscious at this point — and they battle. It is this conflict in consciousness, these battles that are going on (the conscious mind wanting one thing and the subconscious wanting another) that causes most of their symptoms and problems that trigger nervous disorders. They ask questions. They want to know why they are sick, or what the doctor has to say — and they listen to it. They read books on it. They educate the mind. They want an evaluation. They are the ones who will ask for a second opinion. They want to know how and why. Here again, we are talking about the four-year-old. This is the person who, when sick, drives a doctor berserk! They are in a position to help heal themselves, too; and if they think that the doctor knows what he is doing (based on their own evaluation) they will help with the process. They are not just going to lie there!

These people will push themselves and see if they can recover without pain medication, they will exercise a little bit more too. They respond to treatments that require discipline, like exercise, or counseling, or anything in which they can participate. They are willing to take some responsibility for themselves and they can be taught to stay well some of the time. These are people who have a much better chance of being well.

Between three-and-one-half and four-and-one-half people border on independent spirituality. They are less emotional, less dependent on family and friends. Marriage is often confining. They are not as ambitious economically any more, and may choose to have basic skill jobs so as to be free to pursue higher goals. They are rather inclined to peace and leisure, are concept oriented, intellectually developed and motivated, serving common idealistic causes and being health conscious.

From the subconscious age level four-and-a-half and up, qualities of leadership are predominant. The person is highly motivated, healthy, intelligent, educated, conscious, altruistic, idealistic and may become spiritually motivated.

When the subconscious age level is between four and five, such people get sick under special stresses, or when they forget their training if they have had training to stay well. They do not get rattled with little things. They do not let their relatives back them into a corner and tell them they have cancer. But if there is something special — true to their heart — that goes wrong, or an unexpected tragedy occurs,they may get sick as a result. These people can be taught to stay well most of the time. Even when they are sick, they are reluctant to use drugs, and they usually accept only very conservative treatment. They are very willing to help themselves, often to the point where they say: "I am going to get myself well." Even when they accept help, it is of a different nature. They will participate in their treatment and they usually get well and stay well.

The subconscious age level between five and six is not really subject to any particular illnesses. They get sick if they slip in their training, if they become involved with the wrong crowd that keeps them unusually unconscious, but they can be taught to stay well all the time. If they slip, they can usually heal themselves. They do not want any help from anyone. Often they take care of the sick. They are often in the areas served by those in the healing arts and they have insight into what makes sick people "tick." After all, by the time one gets to the age level of five to six years old, one can control others.

At the age between six and seven of the subconscious health is a nearly inviolable rule. It would be very unusual to get sick except for extremely brief periods, and at a very mild degree. In any case, the individual would be able to overcome it quickly by his or her own mind power.

As we have seen, consciousness is the bottom line in health. Consciousness is our best and only healer. A warning is in order. One cannot simply ignore all the early steps and treat oneself or someone else on a much older level. That does not work. The subconscious will not be able to deal with this. One does not just overstep. If the person is two years old or two-and-a-half years old, you cannot just say, "This is simply in your head. Do it yourself," and walk away. They may die because they are really not in a position to do so. We cannot simply force them to accept this. Health professionals must be sure that they know their patient before "pushing" him, before suggesting things that are a little higher than what he is used to. Just reaching a little bit higher, still within his or her comfort zone, is the answer to this, and I am saying his or her comfort zone. The biggest mistake some health professionals and teachers make is to teach those who do not have the maturity or training to understand what they are teaching. No practical use can come from misunderstanding.

The same thing is true with treatment. In treatment as in teaching, you look where you are. Hopefully, you are a few steps ahead of them, and you can then bring them what they need on their level — with perhaps a bit more for them to grow on. They now can grow into the next step. The younger the subconscious the more concrete should be the methods of treatment, including organic therapies such as drugs and in certain situations even surgery, because seeing is believing. The older the subconscious the more abstract could be the methods of therapy such as counseling for self-help, proper dieting, exercise and relaxation. Therefore, in our society where the subconscious average age is about three and one quarter year old, *prevention* gains and will continue to gain more representation in medicine. Certainly crisis medicine, which comprises hardly three percent of the total patients population, will continue to grow more in its sophistication. Holistic health, self-help groups, and emergency will continue to thrive in the years to come.

The subconscious development to higher age levels can be speeded up by proper and special exercises of conscious awakening to awareness, such as different types of meditation, dialogue with the subconscious, and other special techniques which cannot be learned from books; however, under expert supervision, the individual is perhaps enabled to see and understand clearly himself and the world around him better. He may then grasp the purpose of existence, the supreme goal, the Higher Self which is G-d within. This is divine wisdom, love and peace. Then, perhaps, there really will be peace on earth.

A DIRECTORY OF SOME PHILIPPINE HEALERS

(This list does not constitute an endorsement of any of these healers, nor a guarantee that names and addresses are still valid, at the time of this new book edition.)

I.   Faith Healers / Psychic Surgeons

AGAID, ROSITA
Rosales, Pangasinan

ALCANTARA, ANTONIO
Corner Jose Yulo & Ponce Sts.
BF Executive Village
BF Homes, Paranaque, Metro Manila
Tel. No. 828-8926

ASUIGUI, MARECELINO
10 Morning Glory St.
Baguio City

BALACANO, BENJIE
30 P. Paterno St. (Near Banawe)
Quezon City

BLANCE, JUAN
56 Dr. Pilapil St.
Pasig, Metro Manila

BUGARIN, ROMEO
502 Lt. Artiaga St.
San Juan, Metro Manila
Tel. No. 70-50-26

DAVID, MIKE
c/o Mountain Lodge, Baguio City

EMING, ROSITA
36 Valenzuela St.
Baguio City 0201
Tel. No. 52-32

FLORES, JUANITO
402 Nangkaysan
Bacag
Pangasinan

GUITERREZ, VIRGILIO
12 Langka St.
Project 2
Quezon City
Tel. No. 96-16-70

JIMENEZ, RUDY
c/o International Spiritual Center
Barrio Lugnab
Baguio City
Tel. No. 69-06

LABO, JUN
Terraces Hotel
Bavguio City

LAFORGA, EMILIO
Tiza St. Labangon
Cebu City

NACES, FILOMENA
Bo. Vacante
Binalonan, Pangasinan

MERCADO, JOSE (deceased)
c/o Christian Travel Service
Bayview Plaza Hotel
Roxes Blvd., Manila

OLIGANE, DAVID
Bo. Taboy
Asingan, Pangasinan

ORBITO, ALEX
9 Maryland St.
Cubao, Quezon City
Tel. No. 98-59-30

ORBITA, MARCOS
50 Maria Clara St.
Quezon City
Tel. No. 98-62-61

ORBITO, ROGER
9 Maryland St.
Cubao, Quezon City
Tel. No. 98-59-30

PALITAYAN, PLACIDO
10 Palma St.
Baguio City
Tel. No. 37-05

SISON, JOSEPHINE
Villasis, Pangasinan

TERTE, ELEUTERIO (Deceased)
San Fabian, Pangasinan

II.   Magnetic/ Etheric Healers

LOTUACO,BEN
Rugino Ave.
Tahanan Cillage
Paranague, Metro Manila

CU UNJIENG, CHITA
Victoria Court
Harrizon Blvd.
Pasay City

RIVA DE LA, MAGGIE
c/o Success Systems, Inc.
Salcedo Mansions Building
Makati, Metro Manila

SUPNET, FRANCISCO (Ret. Maj.)
2 Maryhurst St.
Baguio City
Tel. No. 49-07

ZALDIVAR, MEL
Bo. Pinagbuhatan
Pasig, Metro Manila

III.   Reflexologists, Bone Setters
       and Physical Therapists

CORDERO, ADELARDO
1414 Blvd.
Roxas Blvd.
Manila

COOPER,ANNETTE
c/o Zen Shisheido
Ermita, Manila

PEREZ,CLETO
Room 1, Victoria Apt.
General Luna, Manila

NOTES

1. R.H.M. Elwes, *Philosophy of Benedict de Spinoza,* (New York: Tudor Publishing Company, 1933), p. 1-3.
2. S. Radhakrishnan, *Eastern Religions and Western Thought,* (London: Oxford University Press, 1939), P.16.
3. Edward Conze, translator, *Buddhist Scriptures* (Baltimore: Penguin Classics, 1959), pp. 19-20.
4. Isaac Meyer, *Qabbalah,* (New York: Stanley Weiser, 1970), p. 171 5. E.G. Browne, *The Literary History of Persia* (Cambridge: Cambridge University Press, 1928).
6. M. K. Misra, *Reincarnation and Islam,* (Madras, 1927), pp. 55-56.
7. *Theosophy Magazine,* September, 1946, pp. 437-38.
8. *Time,* February 4, 1946.
9. Charles Eastmen, *The Soul of the Indian,* (Boston: Houghton Mifflin Co., 1911), p. 167.
10. E. D. Walker, *Reincarnation, A Study of Forgotten Truth,* (New York: University Books, 1965), pp. 335-36.
11. Alfred Bertholet, *Transmigration of Souls,* (New York: Harper & Bros., 1909), pp. 105-08.
12. E. S. Shuckburgh, translator, *Classical Library,* (Cambridge: Harvard University Press, Vol. IX, 1935), pp. 72-74.
13. William A. MacDevitt, translator, *Gallic War,* Book VI, p. 14.
14. William James, *The Will to Believe and Human Immortality,* (New York: Dover, 1956), pp. v-ix.
15. Sigmund Freud, *The Complete Works of Sigmund Freud,* (London: Hogarth Press, 1957), pp. 289-95.
16. Ludwig Binswanger, *Being in the World,* (New York: Basic Books, 1963), p. 4.
17. C. G. Jung, *Memories, Dreams, and Reflections,* (New York: Pantheon Press, 1963), p. 323-33.
18. Richard Wilhelm and C. G. Jung, translators, *The Secret of the Golden Flower,* (New York: Harcourt, Brace and Janovich, 1970), p. 124.
19. C. G. Jung, *Collected Works,* New York: Pantheon, 1959, Vol. 9, Part I *Archetypes and the Collective Unconscious,* pp. 113, 116-17.
20. Edward Tylor, *Religion in Primitive Culture* (Magnolia, Me.: Peter Smith, 1958) p. 103.

21. Ian Stevenson, *Twenty Cases Suggestive of Reincarnation*, Charlottesville, Va.: University Press of Virginia, 1980).

22. "Was it Reincarnation," *American Magazine*, July, 1915.

23. Arthur Guirdhan, *Cathars and Reincarnation* (Wheaton, Ill.: Theosophical Publishing House, 1978).

24. Sunday *Express*, London, May 26, 1935 (interview with M. Martin of Liverpool).

25. Thomas Alva Edison, *Diary and Sundry Observations*, Dagobert Runes, editor, (Westport, Conn.: Greenwood Press).

26. J. B. Rhine, "Did You Live Before," *American Weekly*, April 8, 1956.

27. Helen Wambach, *Reliving Past Lives: The Evidence Under Hypnosis*, (New York: Bantam Books, 1979).

28. Dick Sutphen, *You Were Born Again to be Together*, (New York: Pocket Books, 1978).

29. *Raymond Moody, Life After Life*, (New York: Bantam Books, 1976).

30. Joan Hodgson, *Reincarnation Through the Zodiac*, Vancouver, Washington, (CRCS Publications, 1978).

31. Martin Shulman, *The Moon's Nodes and Reincarnation*, Vol. I (New York: Samuel Weiser, Inc.) 198 1.

32. Max Freedom Long, *The Secret Science at Work*, (Marina del Rey, CA.: DeVorss & Co., 1981), pp. 14-32.

33. Delores Krieger, *The Therapeutic Touch: How to Use Your Hands to Help or to Heal*, (Englewood Cliffs, N.J.: Prentice-Hall, 1979).

34. Jaime T. Licauco, *The Truth Behind Faith Healing in the Philippines*. (National Book Store Publishers, Metro Manila, Philippines, 1981).

35. Lyall Watson, *The Romeo Error*, (London: Coronet Books, 1976).

36. Hiroshi Motoyama, *Tony Agpaoa Psychic Surgery and Its Mechanism*, (Tokyo: Institute for Religious Psychology, 1978).

37. Sladek, Marti, *Two Weeks With Psychic Surgeons*, (Chicago: Doma Press, 1976), pp. 85-87.

38. David St. Claire, *Psychic Healers*, (New York: Bantam Books, 1979), pp. 84-85.

39. Landis, Dylan. *A Scan for Mental Illness* (Discovery Magazine, Oct. 1980), pp. 26-28.

40. Stanley Krippner and Daniel Rubin, editors. The *Kirlian Aura, Photographing the Galaxies of Life* (Anchor Press/ Doubleday, Garden City: New York, 1974), front cover and p. 195.

BIBLIOGRAPHY

Bertholet, Alfred. *Transmigration of Souls.* New York: Harper & Bros., 1909.

Binswanger, Ludwig. *Being in the World.* New York: Basic Books, 1963.

Browne, E. G. *The Literary History of Persia.* Cambridge: Cambridge University Press, 1928.

Conze, Edward. *Buddhist Scriptures.* Baltimore: Penguin Classics, 1959.

Eastmen, Charles. *The Soul of the Indian.* Boston: Houghton Mifflin Co., 1911.

Edison, Thomas Alva. *Diary and Sundry Observations.* Edited by Dagobert Runes. Westport, Conn.: Greenwood Press.

Freud, Sigmund. *The Complete Works of Sigmund Freud.* London: Hogarth Press, 1957.

Guirdham, Arthur, *Cathars and Reincarnation.* Wheaton, Il.: Theosophical Publishing House, 1978.

Joseph Head & S.L. Cranston, *Reincarnation: The Phoenix Fire Mystery*, Warner Books, New York, N.Y. 1979.

Hodgson, Joan. *Reincarnation through the Zodiac.* CRCS Publications, Vancouver, Washington, 1978)

James, William. *The Will to Believe and Human Immortality.* New York: Dover.

Jung, C. G. *Collected Works*, New York, Pantheon, 1959, Vol. 9, Part 1: *Archetypes and the Collective Unconscious.*

Jung, C. G. *Memories, Dreams and Reflections.* New York: Pantheon Press, 1963.

Krieger, Delores. *The Therapeutic Touch: How to Use Your Hands to Help or to Heal.* Englewood Cliffs, N.J.: Prentice-Hall, 1979.

Krippner, Stanley and Rubin, Daniel, editors. *The Kirlian Aura: Photographing the Galaxies of Life*, Anchor Press / Doubleday, Garden City: New York, 1974

Landis, Dylan. *A Scan For Mental Illness*, Discover, Oct. 1980.

Licauco, Jamie T. *The Truth Behind Faith Healing in the Philippines*, National Book Store Publishers, Metro Manila, Philippines, 1981.

Long, Max Freedom. *The Secret Science at Work.* Marina del Rey, CA.: DeVorss & Co., 1981.

MacDevitt, William A., trans. *Gallic War,* Book VI.

Meyer, Isaac. *Qabbalah.* New York: Stanley Weiser, 1970.

Misra, M. D. *Reincarnation and Islam.* Madras, 1927.

Moody, Raymond. *Life After Life.* New York: Bantam Books, 1976.

Motoyama, Hiroshi. *Tony Agpaoa's Psychic Surgery and its Mechanism.* Tokyo: Institute for Religious Psychology, 1978.

Rhine, J. B. "Did You Live Before." *American Weekly,* April 8, 1956.

St. Claire, David. *Psychic Healers.* New York: Bantam Books, 1979.

Shuckburgh, E. S., trans. *Classical Library,* Vol. IX. Cambridge: Harvard University Press, 1935.

Shulman, Martin. *The Moon's Nodes and Reincarnation.* Vol. 1, New York: N.Y. Samuel Weiser, Inc., 1981.

Sladek, Marti. *Two Weeks with the Psychic Surgeons,* Chicago: Doma Press, 1976,

Stevenson, Ian. *Twenty Cases Suggestive of Reincarnation.* Charlottesville, Va.: University Press of Virginia, 1980.

Sutphen, Dick. *You Were Born Again to be Together.* Pocket Books, New York, N.Y. 1978.

Tylor, Edward. *Religion in Primitive Culture.* Magnolia Me.: Peter Smith, 1958.

Walker, E. D. *Reincarnation, A Study of Forgotten Truth.* New York: University Books, 1965.

Wambach, Helen. *Reliving past Lives: The Evidence Under Hypnosis.* New York: Bantam Books, 1979.

Watson, Lyall. *The Romeo Error.* London: Coronet Books, 1976.

Wilhelm, Richard and Jung, C.G., trans. *The Secret of the Golden Flower.* New York: Harcourt, Brace and Janovich, 1970.

ADRIAN FINKELSTEIN, M.D.

Dr. Adrian Finkelstein is assistant clinical professor of psychiatry at the University of California, Los Angeles, and is also on staff of Cedars-Sinai Medical Center in Los Angeles, California. He is former Chairman of Outpatient Department of Psychiatry at Mount Sinai Medical Center, University of Health Sciences, in Chicago, Illinois.

Dr. Finkelstein received his M.D. at Hebrew University, Hadassah Medical School, Jerusalem, then took residency and fellowship training at the Menninger School of Psychiatry, Topeka, Kansas, where, upon graduation in 1972, he received the first Distinguished Award for his research paper titled, "The Relationship between Dreams and Symptoms under Hypnotic, Post-Hypnotic and Natural Conditions." That same year, his paper was honored with the A.E. Bennett Distinguished Award by the Central Neuropsychiatric Association at their 50th Annual Convention in Topeka. Dr. Finkelstein is a member of the American Medical Association and is board-certified by the American Board of Psychiatry and Neurology. He is a member of the American Holistic Medical Association and is listed in Marquis's Who's Who.

For the past 29 years, Dr. Finkelstein has subspecialized in hypnosis and its medical and psychiatric applications. During the past seventeen years, he has been doing research into past lives and past-life therapy, and has been researching and practicing psychic and spiritual healing and their application in the contemporary holistic medical field.

To expand acceptance for holistic health care, his research has led him to Asia, Europe and Mexico. Holistic health care, an alternative medical approach, considers the person as a whole seeking to realign the body, the emotions, the mind and the spirit.

Dr. Finkelstein has appeared many times on television and radio, and been the subject of various newspaper articles. His seminars are particularly pertinent today, for they deal with ways to cope with stress in a rapidly changing, workaholic society, over which hangs an additional fear of annihilation, as people are alienating and distancing from themselves and others, and especially from G-d, due to the rampant growth of the will to receive for oneself alone, selfishly and egotistically. This is the breeding ground for hatred, illness, violence, wars and all negativity.

Coming back to G-d, loving G-d, oneself and each other is the prescription he recommends to the helping professions to use for themselves and the world at large for lasting healing and total fulfillment. He sees this as a marriage between the ancient and contemporary and between the Eastern and Western medical practices, philosophies and traditions.